KidCoder™ Series

KidCoder™: Game Programming

Student Textbook

Second Edition

Copyright 2010

Homeschool Programming, Inc.

KidCoder™: Game Programming

Second Edition

Copyright © 2010 by Homeschool Programming, Inc

ISBN: **978-0-9830749-1-5**

Terms of Use

This course is copyright protected. Copyright 2010 © Homeschool Programming, Inc. Purchase of this course constitutes your agreement to the Terms of Use. You are not allowed to distribute any part of the course materials by any means to anyone else. You are not allowed to make it available for free (or fee) on any other source of distribution media, including the Internet, by means of posting the file, or a link to the file on newsgroups, forums, blogs or any other location. You may reproduce (print or copy) course materials as needed for your personal use only.

Disclaimer

Homeschool Programming, Inc, and their officers and shareholders, assume no liability for damage to personal computers or loss of data residing on personal computers arising due to the use or misuse of this course material. Always follow instructions provided by the manufacturer of 3rd party programs that may be included or referenced by this course.

Contact Us

You may contact Homeschool Programming, Inc. through the information and links provided on our website: http://www.HomeschoolProgramming.com. We welcome your comments and questions regarding this course or other related programming courses you would like to study!

Other Courses

Homeschool Programming, Inc. currently has two product lines for students: the KidCoder™ series and the TeenCoder™ series. Our KidCoder™ series provides easy, step-by-step programming curriculum for 4th through 8th graders. These courses use Visual Basic to teach introductory programming concepts in a fun, graphical manner. Our TeenCoder™ series provides introductory programming curriculum for high-school students. These courses are college-preparatory material designed for the student who may wish to pursue a career in Computer Science or enhance their transcript with a technical elective.

3rd Party Copyrights

This course uses Microsoft's Visual Basic 2010 Express as the programming platform. Visual Studio, Visual Studio Express, Windows, and all related products are copyright Microsoft Corporation. Please see http://www.microsoft.com/express/default.aspx for more details.

Table of Contents

Before You Begin

Please read the following topics before you begin the course.

Minimum Hardware and Software Requirements

This is a hands-on programming course. You will be installing Microsoft's Visual Basic 2010 Express software on your computer. Your computer must meet the following minimum requirements in order to run Visual Basic 2010 Express:

Computer Hardware

Your computer must meet the following minimum specifications:

	Minimum
CPU	1.6GHz or faster processor
RAM	1024 MB
Display	1024 x 768 Direct-X compatible video card
Hard Disk Speed	5400 RPM or faster
Hard Disk Size	3GB available space
DVD Drive	DVD-ROM drive

Operating Systems

Your computer operating system must match one of the following:

Windows XP (x86) with Service Pack 3 or above
Windows Vista (x86 and x64) with Service Pack 2 or above
Windows 7 (x86 and x64)
Windows Server 2003 (x86 and x64) with Service Pack 2 or above
Windows Server 2003 R2 (x86 and x64)
Windows Server 2008 (x86 and x64) with Service Pack 2 or above
Windows Server 2008 R2 (x64)

Conventions Used in This Text

This course will use certain styles (fonts, borders, etc) to highlight text of special interest.

```
Source code will be in 11-point Consolas font, in a single box like this.
```

Variable names will be in **12-point Consolas bold** text, similar to the way they will look in your development environment. For example: **myVariable**.

Function and subroutine names, properties, and keywords will be in **bold face** type, so that they are easily readable.

 This picture highlights important concepts within a lesson.

 Sidebars may contain additional information, tips, or background material.

 A chapter review section is included at the end of each chapter.

 Every chapter includes a "Your Turn" activity that allows you to practice the ideas you have learned in a real program.

What You Will Learn and Do In This Course

KidCoder^TM: Game Programming will teach you how to write your own computer games! This course is designed for students who have already completed the *KidCoder^TM: Windows Programming* introductory course.

Computer game programming, as you might imagine, is a very large subject. There are many different games you can play, and many different programming skills are needed to make those games. Some game programs are simple, while others may take many years and many programmers to make.

This course will build on your Visual Basic programming skills learned in the first *KidCoder^TM: Windows Programming* course. You will learn some simple game programming techniques and apply those to several games. At the end of the course you will know enough to create your own games! Of course your games will not be as complex as the fancy games you can buy in the store today. But these lessons are your first step in understanding the exciting world of computer game programming! Once you understand the basics, you can use your imagination to create many exciting things!

What You Need to Know Before Starting

You are expected to already know the basics of computer use before beginning this course. You need to know how to use the keyboard and mouse to select and run programs, use application menu systems, and work with the Windows operating system. You should understand how to store and load files on your hard disk, and how to use the Windows Explorer to walk through your file system and directory structures. You should also have some experience with using text editors and using web browsers to find helpful information on the Internet.

You should have also completed *KidCoder^TM: Windows Programming* and understand the Visual Basic lessons covered in that course. You should already have installed the Microsoft Visual Basic 2010 Express development environment on your computer. If you are using a new computer then you can find installation instructions in the student files.

Software Versions

You will be using the *Microsoft Visual Basic 2010 Express* software for this course. This program can be freely downloaded from Microsoft's website. Your course will contain download and install instructions in PDF format. Microsoft may from time to time change their website or download process or release newer versions of the product. Please see http://www.HomeschoolProgramming.com for the latest instructions!

Course Errata

We welcome your feedback regarding any course details that are unclear or that may need correction. You can find a list of course errata for this edition on our website.

Chapter One: Getting Started

Welcome to the *KidCoder*^{TM}*: Game Programming* course! This course will teach you how to create your own computer games using the Visual Basic programming language. In this chapter we will review what you learned in the previous course, talk about some different types of games, and look ahead to the lessons in the remaining chapters.

Lesson One: What You Already Know

You should have already completed the introductory *KidCoder*^{TM}*: Windows Programming* course. That course introduced you to computer programming and the Visual Basic programming language. Without a good understanding of the first course, you will have difficulty completing the game programming lessons.

In this lesson we will review some key computer programming ideas and the Visual Basic programming language that you have already learned. If you are not comfortable with any of these topics, we recommend you review the *KidCoder*^{TM}*: Windows Programming* material first before continuing to the game programming lessons!

This lesson is just a brief review of the concepts that you learned in the *KidCoder*^{TM}*: Windows Programming* course. You should know these concepts before attempting the *KidCoder*^{TM}*: Game Programming* course!

Computer Hardware and Software

You should understand the major parts of your computer's hardware and software. The term *hardware* refers to all the physical parts of the computer system. Hardware includes your motherboard, hard drive, memory, video card and sound card. Add-on components (peripherals) such as keyboard, monitor, printer and mouse provide ways for the user to input data and get output data from the computer.

Software is the term for programs that run on computer hardware to make it perform useful tasks. Software can be grouped into three main types of programs: Operating Systems, Device Drivers, and Applications.

Programming Languages

In this course we will be using the Visual Basic programming language. Visual Basic is one of the modern *high-level* programming languages. This language allows you to use English-like words and phrases to tell a computer what tasks to perform. Visual Basic is very powerful yet easy to learn and use at a beginner level.

Visual Studio Express Development Environment

The main software package that we will be using in this course is Microsoft *Visual Basic 2010 Express*. This program is also called an IDE (Integrated Development Environment). The IDE is a single place where you can create your screens, type in your code, and run and debug your program. Everything you need as a programmer can be found in your IDE.

You learned how to use the Visual Basic 2010 Express IDE in the introductory course. At this point you should be comfortable working with Visual Basic programs in that environment. If you do not yet have the IDE installed on your computer, you will get a chance to install the software at the end of this chapter.

Compiling and Running your Programs

After writing your program code you will *compile* it into an executable - a file ending in .EXE. You can then run the executable and even debug it from within the IDE.

To compile and run a project that is open in the IDE, you can use the "play" ▶ button on the toolbar, hit the F5 key, or click on "Debug" and then "Start Debugging" on the menu bar. All three of these options will perform the same action: a compile to check for errors in the program and, if there are no errors, your program will begin running.

Any errors that occur while compiling your program will show up in the "Error" window in the bottom of your screen. The program will not run if the Visual Basic Express software found any errors.

Data Types and Variables

Most useful programs require data to work. A calculator application needs numbers to calculate, an MP3 player needs music files to play, and an image editor needs pictures to load. In programming, data is handled in your program by named *variables*. Each variable has a data type that can hold a certain kind of data.

The most common types of data are numeric (**Integer, Double, Decimal**) or character data (**Char, String**). A **Boolean** data type holds either the value **True** or **False**.

Program Flow Control with If/Else and For/While Loops

Flow control means making decisions in your program about what statements to run. You can use *logical expressions* which evaluate to **True** or **False** to make a decision. Logical expressions always result in either **True** or **False**, like "If the number of students is greater than 5". *Relational operators* are used to compare two pieces of data or two expressions that produce data. The relational operators are: **<** (less than), **>** (greater than), **=** (equal to), and **<>** (not equal to).

The **If** statement is a line of code that tests a logical expression. If the expression evaluates to **True**, the program will execute some statements within the **If** block. An **If** statement can include any number of **ElseIf** statements to test other logical expressions if the last test was **False**. The last part of the **If** statement can be an **Else** statement, which will only execute if all of the other logical expressions are **False**.

Sometimes you will want your program to execute the same group of statements more than once. For example, you may want a program to print out the names and test scores for 10 students. This program would need a series of statements that printed the students' first name, last name and test score. We could write a set of these statements for each student, but that would mean a lot of repeated code. Instead what we will do is *loop* through one set of statements 10 times. The loops that we will use are the **For** loop and the **While** loop. The **For** loop executes the statements a known number of times. The **While** loop will execute the statement *while* some logical expression is true.

Receiving and Validating User Input

User input is a very important part of programming. Most programs will need some way to receive data or directions from the user.

In Visual Basic, an **InputBox** is a great way to quickly and easily get a single piece of information from a user. These boxes are pop-up windows that allow a user to answer a single question.

To get more than one piece of information from a user, you will need to create a custom "Form", which is a window in Visual Basic. You can place one or more Textbox controls on the form along with descriptive labels that tell the user what data to enter in the fields. Within your code you can then get the user's data by reading the **.Text** properties of the Textbox control variables on the form.

Validating user input is an important task to make sure the data entered by a user is what the program expects. Some common functions used in data validation are the **IsNumeric()** and **Val()** functions, which help to make sure that strings contain only numbers or the right numeric values. To see if a user has left a Textbox blank, you can just check to see if the **.Text** property is equal to an empty string ("").

Math Operations and Working with Numbers

Math operators are the symbols that we use to do mathematical calculations, like adding, subtracting, multiplying and dividing. Visual Basic (and just about every other programming language) uses these special characters to perform the math operations:

+	Addition
-	Subtraction
*	Multiplication
/	Division

Visual Basic contains some pre-written functions which help to perform math tasks, like calculating square roots (with the **Sqr()** function) or finding absolute values (with the **Abs()** function).

Sometimes a programmer may need to convert from one data type to another. Visual Basic contains some common conversion functions you may find useful. For example, the **Str()** function is used to convert a number to a string, and the **Val()** function is used to convert a string to a number.

Math Shortcuts

There are many times when you want to use a variable in an expression and then store the result of the expression in the same variable. For example, you may want to add 1 to your variable, or subtract 2 from your variable, etc. You can write out the full statements like this:

```
Dim i As Integer = 5
i = i + 1
i = i - 2
i = i * 4
i = i / 2
```

These statements can be a little boring to type out each time, especially when your variable name is long. Instead, you can use a cool little shortcut by combining the math operator with the equals sign. Here are the statements above, re-written with the shortcut style:

```
Dim i As Integer = 5
i += 1              // same as i = i + 1
i -= 2              // same as i = i - 2
i *= 4              // same as i = i * 4
i /= 2              // same as i = i / 2
i += (4 * 3 - 2)    // same as i = i + (4 * 3 - 2)
```

Notice how much simpler the statements are with the shortcuts! We will use these shortcuts often in our game programs.

Working with Strings

The **String** data type is used to hold a line of text or group of characters. There are many common library functions that deal with strings. You can change the letters in a string to upper-case (**UCase**()), or change the letters to lower case (**LCase**()), or even reverse the order of the string (**StrReverse**()).

Using the Debugger

A *debugger* will let you walk step-by-step through each line in your program and watch your program as it runs. This is an extremely powerful tool. While you are looking at the running program, you can make sure the program is working as you expect. This includes making sure the statements are executing in the correct order and even watching the contents of your variables to make sure the data is being stored correctly.

Using Functions and Subroutines

Functions and subroutines are groups of program statements that execute each time you "call" them. In Visual Basic a subroutine is abbreviated as **Sub**. The only difference between a **Function** and a **Sub** is that **Functions** will return a data value when it is finished executing, while **Subs** cannot return values. You may pass any number and type of data parameters to both **Functions** and **Subs**.

Because **Functions** and **Subs** are so much alike, we will generally use the word "function" to describe either a **Function** or a **Sub** when it doesn't really matter which type we're talking about!

Lesson Two: Types of Computer Games

Computer games have been around for almost as long as computers themselves. In fact, modern computers got their start around the mid 1940s, and by 1952, the first computer game was being played. The game was just simple tic-tac-toe, and it probably ran on a computer that was about the same size as your house, but it was a game!

Over the years computer games have improved from text-based games, to simple arcade graphics of the 1970s, to the more complicated Atari and Nintendo games of the 80s, to the complex, graphics-intense games of today's personal computers and consoles. As computer games evolved, many different *types* of games became available. The variety of possible computer games is only limited by human imagination. If you can dream it, chances are you can create it!

In this lesson, we will discuss some of the more common types of computer games:

- Arcade games
- Board games
- Role Playing Games (RPG)
- Sports simulators
- Real Time Strategy (RTS)
- First Person Shooter (FPS)
- Massively Multiplayer Online RPG (MMORPG)

Arcade Games

Arcade games began in the 1970s and quickly became very popular. These games were housed in big, upright arcade cabinets and required money to play. The first successful arcade game was a game called Pong, which was a two-player, tennis-like game where each player moved a "paddle" to try to hit a ball back-and-forth. The graphics were very simple: the "paddle" was just a vertical bar on the screen and the "ball" was a small square dot. You have already created your own simple version of Pong as the final project in the *KidCoder™: Windows Programming* course!

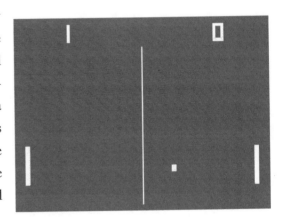

Atari's Pong game from 1979

Arcade games are still popular today. Many different arcade games include themes such as auto racing, fighting, shooting, sports, fantasy, space ships, aliens, food fights, angry gorillas, etc.

Board Games

Another popular type of computer game is the board game. Some games are just computerized versions of popular table games, like Chess, Checkers, and Othello. These games usually consist of a top-down view of the game board. Players take turns rolling the dice, moving the pieces and following the rules for the space that they have landed on. These games tend to be popular year after year since everyone knows how to play them. Other types of computer board games are completely new and creative with no real-world example.

Role Playing Games

Some of the most popular computers games are the "Role Playing Games" or RPGs. In these games, a player will assume the identity of one or more characters and will make them interact with a virtual world over a long period of time. Fantasy games might have swords, wizards and monsters, while real-world games try to copy real life or history, and science fiction games might use space ships, other planets and aliens. The graphics of these games can range from simple text-only displays to very realistic 3D graphics.

Sports Simulators

Sports simulation games allow you to "play" sports like football, baseball, basketball, golf, snow skiing, or racing. These games usually have realistic graphics that make you feel as if you are playing on the field in real life. Sports games rely on a programming concept called "game physics". Game physics make a ball or puck "bounce" in a realistic way, or make a car drive on a road in a realistic manner, or make snow spray around your skis as if you were really on the slopes. We will talk more about game physics in a later chapter.

Real Time Strategy

Real-Time Strategy games or RTS games are fast-paced games in which players move a large number of game pieces around in the environment without taking turns! In these games, you and your opponents all play in real-time, which mean you are all attempting to achieve the same result at the same time. You may try to build an empire by planting cities, building military and civilian units, and gathering resources like stone, gold or wheat. Once you have built your empire, you can move your military or civilian units across the landscape in a strategic manner and attempt to defeat one or more opponents. You must act quickly and juggle a number of tasks at the same time in order to defeat your opponents or they will overcome you!

First Person Shooter

A very popular type of game developed within the last couple of decades is the "First Person Shooter" (or FPS) game. These games usually offer the highest performance 3-Dimensional (3D) graphics. The term "first person" means you are looking out into the world as if through the eyes of a person. The games tend to span many different levels filled with monsters, aliens, or other opponents. The objective of the game is usually to survive by shooting the bad guys with a variety of splashy weapons.

Massively Multiplayer Online RPG

Massively Multiplayer Online RPGs (MMORPGs) are a recent extension of the traditional RPG. Instead of working individually within a game limited to your own computer, you can play online in a large virtual world with hundreds or thousands of companions. MMORPGs typically require a high speed internet connection and a monthly subscription to pay for the complex game servers run by the game company.

Lesson Three: What You Will Learn In This Course

In the last lesson you learned about some of the different types of computer games. It would be impossible to teach you how to create all of these games in one course. Professional store-bought games are rarely an individual effort; most are created by teams of trained graphic artists, sound artists, and programmers who specialize in different types of programming. However, one smart or energetic person can still write creative and enjoyable games! During this course we will learn some key concepts in game programming. Along the way you will create several real games!

The course topics we will cover include:

Game Design	<ul><li>writing game proposals or designs</li><li>how games should be built around a game engine</li><li>using timers to drive game activity</li></ul>
Screen Coordinates	<ul><li>how to locate something on the screen</li><li>Visual Basic arrays and structures</li><li>drawing simple geometric shapes on the screen with Toolbox controls</li></ul>
User Input	<ul><li>using mouse events</li><li>capturing keyboard events</li></ul>
Graphics and Drawing	<ul><li>painting the screen using the Graphics object</li><li>brushes, pens, and shapes without using Toolbox controls</li></ul>
Images and Animation	<ul><li>animation concepts</li><li>image formats</li><li>creating animation using timers and images</li></ul>
Sprites	<ul><li>wrapping useful graphics objects and commands in a library</li><li>moving sprites on the screen</li><li>collision detection</li></ul>
Sound	<ul><li>creating simple beeps</li><li>playing music and recorded sounds</li></ul>
Artificial Intelligence	<ul><li>artificial intelligence applied to games</li></ul>

Saving Games	• file input and output
	• common file open and file save dialogs
	• saving and loading the game state
Game Physics	• reflection (bouncing)
	• gravity and acceleration
Text and Printing	• drawing text of different sizes, shapes, colors, fonts, and effects
	• printing form screens to the printer

Within each chapter you will be working on a real game that uses the lesson topics! The games that you will create in this course will be pretty cool, but also fairly simple. In the last chapter you will create a final project. The final project will include many of the topics covered in the course.

Chapter Review

- Hardware is the term for all of the physical parts of a computer.

- Software is the term for the programs running on the computer that make it perform useful work

- Software programs can be described as: Operating Systems, Device Drivers, and Applications.

- Visual Basic is a high-level programming language.

- An IDE is an Integrated Development Environment where a programmer can create screens, write code, and debug programs.

- Programs use variables to store numeric, string, and other data types.

- A **String** is a data type that is used to hold a group of characters or line of text.

- Flow control in a program is achieved with **If** statements, **For** loops, and **While** loops.

- User input is very important in game programming. Users need to be able to interact with the game.

- Math operators are symbols used to do mathematical calculations.

- A Debugger is a tool that allows you to walk through a program line-by-line. This makes fixing errors in a program much easier.

- In Visual Basic you can write **Functions** (which return a value) or **Subs** (which do not return a value).

- Some common types of computer games are arcade games, board games, role-playing games, sports simulation games, real-time strategy games, first-person shooter games, and multiplayer online games.

- Most store-bought game programs are the result of many different people with many different skills. These games require graphic artists, sound artists, animators, and programmers.

Your Turn! Install Visual Basic 2010 Express

In this activity you will be installing the course files, the Microsoft Visual Basic 2010 Express software and the MSDN Help Library on your computer.

Course files	The files that come with this course include material for the student (chapter sample programs, activity starters, instructional documents) and for the teacher (activity solutions, tests, answer keys, etc).
Visual Basic 2010 Express	This software is a free student version of the professional Visual Studio product. Visual Studio is a popular example of an IDE, or Integrated Development Environment. This is a very important piece of software for any programmer! An IDE is the central place where you will create, compile, run, and debug your program.
MSDN Help Library	The MSDN Help Library is an integrated reference system that allows programmers to quickly find help on functions and programming concepts from within the IDE.

You may have already installed Visual Basic 2010 Express and the MSDN Help Library on your computer when completing the *KidCoder: Windows Programming* course. In that case you do not have to repeat those steps, just install the course files for *KidCoder: Game Programming*!

Note: If you have installed the Visual Basic 2008 Express software as part of an earlier course edition, you should complete the Visual Basic 2010 installation as this course's projects are based on this newer version!

Installing the Course Files

The files for this course are installed by a single setup executable that came with your course purchase. The setup file is called "KidCoder_GameProgramming.exe" (or similar name). Ensure that you are running a Windows account with administrative privileges on your machine when you launch the setup executable.

The setup executable will offer you the choice of installing the Student Files and/or Solution Files. You may install these components on the same computer (if the student should have free access to the solutions) or on different computers (so the teacher can maintain control over the solutions).

Go ahead and perform this setup process now. We recommend installing to the default "C:\KidCoder\Game Programming" directory as we will refer to that directory structure throughout the textbook. You may choose a different location if you want to. The setup program will automatically create a "My Projects" directory under the target installation – this is where all of the student projects will go!

Once installation is complete you will have a new "KidCoder" group on your Windows Start Menu. Underneath "KidCoder" is a "Game Programming" folder. Within that folder are one or two menus for the Student and Solution files (depending on your choices during setup). The look and feel of the Windows Start Menu changes between versions of Windows, but your final menu system should look something like this (assuming both Student and Solution files installed):

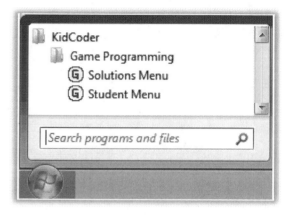

You can run these menus for convenient, graphical access to all of the instructional documents (PDFs), activity solutions, and other material distributed with the course. You may also simply run Windows Explorer and navigate to your target install directory (C:\KidCoder\Game Programming) and launch these files on your own! Use of the Menu systems is optional. Here is an example screen shot from Windows Explorer that shows the directory structure and files in your target directory (details may vary).

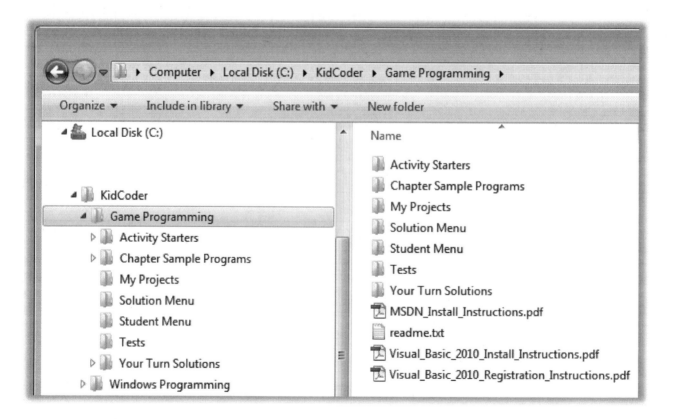

A ".PDF" file is a common document format that requires the free Adobe Acrobat program to read. Your computer should already have the Acrobat reader installed. If you cannot view the PDF documents, you will need to install Acrobat reader first from http://get.adobe.com/reader/.

Installing Visual Basic 2010 Express

Your next major activity is to install the Visual Basic 2010 Express software on your computer. You will need to be connected to the Internet during the installation of Visual Basic 2010 Express. Always ask your teacher before doing any activity online! Now, let's get started!

Your course includes a document named "Visual_Basic_2010_Install_Instructions.pdf" which contains complete, step-by-step instructions on downloading and installing the software.

Please open the "Visual Basic Install Instructions.pdf" document now, either through the Student Menu or by launching the PDF directly from Windows Explorer, and follow the instructions to install the IDE on your computer. Within 30 days of installation you also need to register with Microsoft (a free process), so we recommend you do that now as well. Please read and complete the instructions in the "Visual_Basic_2010_Registration_Instructions.pdf" document to register your software with Microsoft.

Getting Help!

Very often you will want to get help on an error, or function description, or some other part of Visual Studio or the Visual Basic programming language. The MSDN (Microsoft Developer Network) Library, a great help tool, can be installed on top of Visual Studio. Then, to get help on any topic, just position the mouse in the IDE on the item in question (like a compiler error number or function name) and hit the F1 key. If help files are not installed locally, MSDN will go online to get help for you.

Please find the "MSDN_Install_Instructions.pdf" document in your course materials and follow those instructions now to install the MSDN help library.

You can also use many online resources to help find solutions to error messages or understand the meaning of certain Visual Basic topics. Any of the major search engines will lead you to dozens of topics on programming and Visual Studio. Some well-established sites such as Wikipedia (http://www.wikipedia.com) also offer good articles on many programming topics.

The Working Directory for Projects

After installing the course files, a "My Projects" directory was automatically created for you. This directory will be the location where you will save all of your projects for this course. The default directory  structure is "C:\KidCoder\Windows Programming\My Projects". Each project you create should be placed in a new sub-folder within your working directory. You may select a different working directory or even create additional working directories on your own; just remember your directory location when you want to save and load your projects. Multiple students may use the same computer for this course by creating different working directories! Use the Windows Explorer program to create new directories.

Chapter Two: Game Design

In this chapter we will explore some strategies of game design. You will learn how to form game ideas by brainstorming and writing requirements. You will also learn about game engines which are the internal pieces of code and data that make games behave properly. Finally we will review the use of events and timers which are both critical to most game designs.

Lesson One: Game Proposal

The first step in creating a computer game is to plan exactly how you think the game should work: What kind of a game are you creating? What parts are involved? Will it need graphics? Sound? These questions and more will need to be answered before you can sit down with Visual Studio and start programming!

Writing computer games is a more creative process than most types of programs. But you still need to put as much thought and planning into games as you would any business application. To begin, it is a good idea to sit down and *brainstorm* about the major parts of your game. Start with a good game description. This will help solidify your ideas. Try and think about some of the following items:

- What general kind of game do you want to make? Will it be a puzzle game? An arcade game? Or something completely different?
- Put some of your visual ideas on paper by drawing example screens that players will see.
- How will your player control the game? What mouse and keyboard controls will they use?
- Will your game be for one player or multiple players?
- Will your game need any special sounds or graphics?
- Is there a story or other background behind your game that the player should understand first?

These are just "starter" questions. Once you begin answering these questions, you may come up with some others on your own. This brainstorming session is very important to the design of your game. Some features of a game may not be obvious until you start planning. Once you start writing down your ideas, chances are you will find yourself modifying some parts of the game to make others work better.

Your imagination and creativity are some of the most important tools in designing computer games. Brainstorming is a great way to turn creativity into a solid game plan!

Once you have a good idea what your game will be all about, you will need to start thinking about how you will *design* your game. "Designing" a game means planning, in detail, how you will write the code to make your ideas come to life. For example, you can look at the requirements that you have written and then plan the following parts of the code.

Game Data

You must decide what kind of data you will need to track during the game. If your game is keeping a score, you will need a numeric data type to hold this score. If your game will have one or more objects moving around the screen, you will need to keep track of the current locations of your objects. In a multi-player game, you may need to keep track of who has the current "turn" in the game. All of these data needs should be obvious when you look over your game requirements. Make a list of all the data types and purposes in your program.

Game Logic

You will need to think about how the different pieces and components of your game will be controlled. Will you need to move pieces around the screen? Will objects bounce off the edges of the screen? Will there be a time limit on your players? Will your players be shooting at objects? What happens if they hit objects? These questions all address the overall logic of your game.

Timing

You will need to decide if you will need a timer loop in your game. If your game has a time-limit, or if you need to make things happen periodically, or if you need to move or animate objects on the screen, you will probably need at least one timer. On the other hand your game could be completely user-driven and simply wait for user input to move forward.

Baby Steps

Finally, you should plan to write your game in stages so that you can test parts as you go along. Dividing a game program up into smaller parts avoids the "big-bang" programming problem. If you write a complicated program all at once, and then have to compile, run, and debug that program all at once, there will likely be so many little problems that the entire program will go "bang"! It is much easier to break your program into smaller and easier pieces that you can make sure work before moving on to the next step.

Lesson Two: Game Engine

If you have read anything about game programming before, you have probably heard the term: *game engine*. A game engine is a collection of programming code and data that will help to make your game work. Game engines are responsible for everything from drawing the graphics on the screen, to interpreting user input, to managing background tasks such as the computer player's "artificial intelligence".

 **The game engine is the brain of a computer game. This is the part of the program that performs all of the game logic. A solid engine is very important to a quality game!**

Game engines are important for several reasons. First, planning a game engine as a concrete component with well-known parts helps you during the design phase of your program. Knowing that you need a game engine and knowing what parts make up a game engine is often a helpful starting point when you are staring at that first empty source file!

Second, in commercial games the game engine is often re-used in more than one game. Games that are very similar (e.g. two adventure games or two first-person shooters) may use the same game engine under the covers, yet show different graphics and storyline to the user. Being able to share code between more than one program is a great time-saver as you don't have to re-invent the wheel for each program. In this course we will not share game engines between programs because our games are all very different. However we will identify common tasks that are needed in most games and build a library that we will re-use across each game to save us time and energy!

Game engines can be divided into several general sections: game state, game logic, and user interactions.

Game State

The game state is a very important part of a game program. This is the data section of the engine. The game state contains the collection of variables and data that represent everything about the past, present or future state of your game. This section will contain information about who is playing the game, where the game pieces are on the board, how many points or how much money a player has, the position and direction of all the objects in the game, the current player's turn, etc. As you can see there are many pieces of important information in a game. The data section of the game engine helps to manage and control all of this information.

If you want to be able to save your game to disk and resume game play later, it is the data within the game state that must be saved! When you re-load your game state from disk the game can then continue from where it left off.

Game Logic

The controller logic within the game engine applies user input to the game state according to the rules of the game. You can picture this logic as a traffic cop at a busy intersection. Many things are happening at the same time in different directions, and the cop needs to manage the behavior of each car safely through the intersection according to the traffic laws. Your game logic may include:

- Enforcing the rules of the game
- Understanding the user input as a move or command that may affect the current game state
- Direct the overall program flow
- Establish timers to make things happen without user input

User Interactions

The last part of a game engine is the input and output section. This section is responsible for managing the different ways that a user can give input and receive output from a game. Typically, users give input with the mouse or keyboard and get output from the screen graphics or sound effects. Your user input will come in the form of event functions called by the program each time a user clicks the mouse or presses a key. Your user output may go through one or more graphics libraries and the Form's **Paint()** method to display text and graphics to the user, or through a soundcard to play sound effects or music.

Example Game Engine

To give you a better idea of how the game engine pieces will work together, let's take a look at a simple tic-tac-toe game example. The game engine might be implemented as follows:

Game State	The game state would include variables for each of the squares on the tic-tac-toe board. These variables would keep track whether each square was blank or contained an X or O. The game state would also contain a variable to keep track of whose turn it is for the next move.
Game Logic	The controller section of the game engine would contain all of the logic that manages the game play. This section looks at each player's move and determines if it is valid. If a user tries to put an X or an O on the board, the controller will first make sure that the square is blank, and then will update the game state to contain an X or an O in the square. Once the X or O is added, the controller will also check to see if there are 3 Xs or 3 Os in a row, which would complete the game.
User Interactions	Finally, the input and output section would be responsible for accepting user input such as a mouse click on a blank game square. User output would include drawing the game board based on the current game state, and displaying an indication of the current player's turn.

Lesson Three: Events and Timers

Your game will likely rely on events to make things happen. Events may be generated by user input or by periodic timers.

Events

Visual Basic is an event-driven programming language. This means that Visual Basic programs are designed to respond to the events that a user creates while using the program. If a user clicks on a button, the program receives a "Button-Clicked" event. If the user presses a key, the program receives a "Key-Pressed" event. The program then can perform actions based the type of event. For example, if the user pressed the "Exit" button, we can exit the program. If the user pressed the up arrow key, we can move the current object up one space.

The Visual Basic IDE makes it very easy to create functions that respond to events. Once the event handler function is created you just need to write the code within the function that responds to the event. An event handler can be created for a specific event in one of several ways:

The easiest method to create an event for a specific control is to double-click on the control in the form design window. This will create an event handler for the most common event for that control. For example, if you double-click on a button on your form, the IDE will automatically switch to the code window and will create a "Button Click" event handler. If you double-click on the form itself, the code window will open and a "Form Load" event will automatically be created. The "Form Load" event is the most common form-related event.

If you want more control over the event handlers in your program, you will want to create the event handlers in the code window with the drop-down boxes at the top of that window. Here is an example:

The above image shows two drop-down list boxes: the left list box will list the controls available on the form and the right list box will list all of the events that are available for that control. For example, when you drop-down the left list box, it should look something like this:

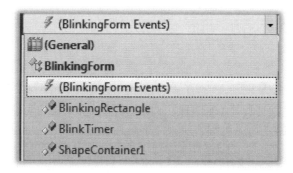

You can see that this form is called **BlinkingForm** and it contains two controls: **BlinkingRectangle** and **BlinkTimer**. You can also choose the option: (**BlinkingForm_Events**), which will allow you to choose events for the form itself. Let's say we choose the **BlinkingRectangle** control. Now the right list box would look like this:

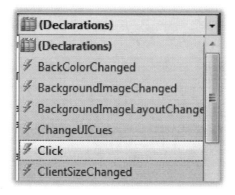

Here, you can see that there are many possible events for the **BlinkingRectangle** control. When an event already contains some code, the event will be displayed in **bold** type.

Now take a look at the highlighted event: **Click**. If we chose the **Click** event from the list, the code window would automatically add the new handler function for this event:

```
    Private Sub BlinkingRectangle_Click(ByVal sender As Object, _
                            ByVal e As System.EventArgs) _
                            Handles BlinkingRectangle.Click

    End Sub
```

There! Now if we wanted to, we could add some code that would be called when someone "clicks" on our blinking rectangle!

Much of our game controller logic will be found in event handler functions. Whenever a user clicks the mouse on the screen, moves the mouse on the screen or hits a key on the keyboard, an event will fire. More game logic can be found in an important event handler that gets called automatically if you set up a timer...we'll talk about that next!

Timers

Timers are a very important part of a Visual Basic game. Timers allow you to create an action that occurs at regular intervals, regardless of whether or not the user is doing anything. Game animation is done using a timer control. For instance, let's say we have a game that allows a ball to bounce around the screen. We cause the ball to move by setting a timer to move the ball a few pixels many times a second. We could also use a timer to move a race car further along on a track, or to update a countdown timer on the screen. Timers are very useful elements in a game!

Timers cause a timer handler function to be called at periodic intervals. The lowest interval is 1 millisecond, or 1 thousandth of a second. A timer that runs every 1 millisecond is running 1000 times per second - extremely fast! Typically, when you want to animate an object, you want a value of around 33 milliseconds. This mimics the rate at which the human eye can see changes in the screen and makes the animation look nice and smooth.

To create a timer in a program, you must first add the Timer control to your form. The Timer control can be found in the "Components" section of your Toolbox.

Once you have added a Timer to the screen, you will notice that it does not show up directly on your form. Instead, it will show up at the bottom of the design window.

This is because the Timer control is not a visible control that can be moved and resized on a form, like a button or a textbox.

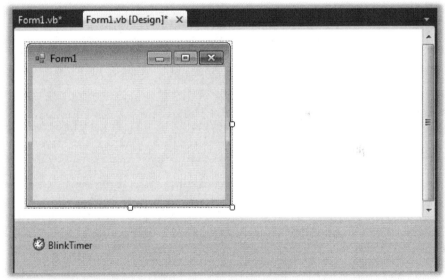

A Timer control has properties, just like any other form control. If you click on the Timer control in the design window and look at the Property Sheet, you will see all of the control's properties. The most important property for a Timer control is the **Interval** property. This is the time, in milliseconds, that the Timer control will wait between firing its event. You can also set the timer **(Name)** to make it more descriptive.

A Timer control has only one function: to fire an event at a specific interval. The event that the Timer control will fire is called the **Tick** event. To add the event handler for the **Tick** event to your program, you can either double-click on the Timer control in the design window, or add the event with the drop-down boxes in the code window. Either way, the resulting event handler will look something like this:

```
Private Sub Timer1_Tick(ByVal sender As System.Object, _
                        ByVal e As System.EventArgs) Handles Timer1.Tick

        ' Tick-handling goes here
End Sub
```

The default control name is "Timer1" but you can change the **(Name)** property on the control, and the event handler function name should change to match. Any code that you enter in the Timer's **Tick** event handler (or the **Tick** function) will be executed every time the Timer fires.

Lesson Four: Blinking Rectangles

In this lesson, we will practice simple animation with timers. To begin, open the Visual Basic 2010 Express IDE and create a new project called "Blinking Rectangle".

Change the name and text of "Form1" by clicking on the form and then finding the **(Name)** and **Text** properties in the Property Sheet. Change the **(Name)** property to **BlinkingForm** and the **Text** property to "Blinking Rectangle".

 Your Visual Basic 2010 Express should already have the "Power Packs" section in your toolbox. Rarely, the Power Packs can be missing for some reason. If you cannot find them, please check the support area of our website for instructions on getting the Power Packs installed!

The first thing we will do in our program is create a rectangle on the screen. Look in the Toolbox for the Visual Basic PowerPacks section. You should find a **RectangleShape** control here. Drag and drop the shape onto your form. Change the name of the shape to **BlinkingRectangle**; change the **FillStyle** to "Solid" and the **FillColor** to any color you want.

You should now see a screen like this one:

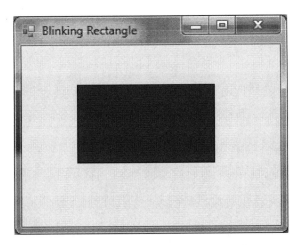

Now you will need to add a Timer control to the form. The Timer control is in the toolbox under the Components section. If you double-click the toolbox timer, you should see the control show up at the bottom of the design window. It will not show on the form itself, because it is not a visible component. Change the name of the timer to **BlinkingTimer** and the interval to 200.

If you double-click on the **BlinkingTimer**, the code window should appear with the **BlinkingTimer Tick** event. We are going to do a simple **If** statement here to check to see if the Rectangle is showing or not. If it is showing, we will hide it, if it is hidden, we will show it. Create your Tick function like this:

```
Private Sub BlinkTimer_Tick(ByVal sender As System.Object, _
                            ByVal e As System.EventArgs)
If (BlinkingRectangle.Visible = False) Then
        BlinkingRectangle.Show()
    Else
        BlinkingRectangle.Hide()
    End If
End Sub
```

Here we are using one Rectangle property: **Visible**, and two Rectangle methods: **Show()** and **Hide()**. If the **BlinkingRectangle** is not displayed on the screen, then its **Visible** property will be set to **False**. If it is showing on the screen, the **Visible** property will be **True**.

Our code checks to see if the **BlinkingRectangle** is not showing. If it is not, we call the **Show()** method to make it visible. If it is already visible, we use the **Hide()** method to hide it from the user. By using the timer to show and hide the Rectangle at regular intervals, we are effectively blinking the rectangle.

The final step in using a Timer control is starting the timer. In order for the timer to "tick", it must be started. One simple place to start a timer is in the "Form Load" event. Any code that exists in this event will be run as the program starts up. To add code to the Form Load event, just double-click anywhere on the form in the Form Design window, or choose "BlinkingForm Events" and "Load" from the Code window. This should display the following screen:

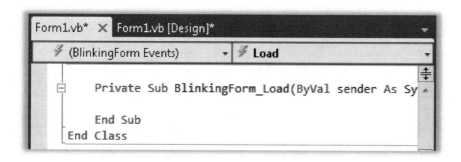

Here we add just one line of code:

```
Private Sub BlinkingForm_Load(ByVal sender As System.Object, _
                          ByVal e As System.EventArgs) Handles MyBase.Load
        BlinkingTimer.Start()
End Sub
```

This line will start the **BlinkingTimer** and cause the **Tick**() event to fire every 200 milliseconds (which is the interval you configured on the Property Sheet).

If you need to stop a timer for any reason (perhaps the game is paused), just call the **Stop**() method on the control and the Tick function will no longer be called. You can **Start**() and **Stop**() a timer control as many times as you need during a game.

Go ahead and try the blinking rectangles program. Experiment with the timer control's interval times. Does a longer interval change the blink rate? Does a short interval make the blinking difficult to see?

 **Chapter Review**

- Game programming requires creativity and imagination

- Game programming requires a great deal of planning and thought.

- Brainstorming is a good way to come up with game ideas.

- Game design is planning how you will implement your game ideas.

- Game engines can be divided into several parts: game state, game logic and user interactions.

- Game state is the data section of the game engine.

- Game logic controls how the game works.

- Visual Basic is an event-driven language.

- Most of the game control logic will be functions that respond to events in the game.

- Timers are very useful in games. Timers allow you to create actions that occur at regular intervals.

Your Turn! Clock Application

For this activity, you will use a timer to create an automatically updated digital clock.

The starter project for this activity can be found in your "**\KidCoder\Game Programming\Activity Starters\Clock**" directory. The name of the solution for this chapter is "**Clock.sln**". Go ahead and start the Visual Basic 2010 Express software and open this solution.

The starter project contains a label control named **TimeLabel**. This will be used to display the current time.

Here are the steps that you need to take to complete this activity:

1. Create a Timer control on your form and name it **ClockTimer**. Set the **Interval** for the **ClockTimer** to fire once per second (an interval value of 1000).

2. Open the code window and find or create the **ClockTimer_Tick** event handler.

3. Within the **Tick** event handler, do the following:
   a. Declare a variable called **currentTime** of data type **DateTime** to hold the current time
   b. Set the variable equal to the current time using the **DateTime.Now** property:

```
Dim currentTime As DateTime = DateTime.Now
```

   c. Set the **TimeLabel.Text** property equal to the current time. You can use the **ToString()** method on the DateTime object with the parameter "hh:mm:ss tt" to create as string with the hours, minutes, seconds, and "AM" or "PM":

```
TimeLabel.Text = currentTime.ToString("hh:mm:ss tt")
```

4. Find or create the event handler for the **Form Load** event.

5. Start the Timer in your Form Load event using the Timer's **Start()** method

Your digital clock program, when run, should now show the current time updated once a second!

Chapter Three: Drawing on the Screen

In this chapter we will begin exploring the graphical concepts you will need to write successful computer games. We review the contents of a screen in terms of colored pixels and coordinates. We also introduce two new data concepts - arrays and structures -- that will greatly simplify your game implementation. Finally you will learn about the basic graphics shapes (circles, lines, rectangles) available in the Form design screen through the Toolbox.

Lesson One: Screen Coordinates

Computer screens are all made of individual dots called pixels. These pixels are arranged on the screen in a grid pattern. You may have heard a screen's size described in terms of its resolution: 640x480, 800x600, or 1024x768. These numbers describe the screen width and height in terms of pixel counts. A screen that has a resolution of 800x600 is displaying a grid of 800 pixels across and 600 pixels down.

Each pixel on a screen is capable of displaying a single color at a time. The actual color can change, depending on what the program wants to display, but a single pixel can only show one color at a time. The grouping of different colored pixels on the screen is what creates the images we see on our computer.

The pixels on the screen are commonly identified by a pair of numbers. These numbers tell how far the pixel is from the left and top of the screen. The distance from the left of the screen is called the "X-coordinate" and the distance from the top of the screen is called the "Y-coordinate". These numbers are typically called a "coordinate pair" and look like this: **(X, Y)**

The upper-left coordinate on a screen is always (0, 0). As you move across the screen, the first number increases. The next pixel over from the upper-left would be (1, 0) and the next would be (2, 0). As you move down the screen, the second number increases. The next pixel down from the upper-left would be (0, 1) and the next down would be (0, 2).

Here is a small grid that shows this concept:

0,0	1,0	2,0
0,1	1,1	2,1
0,2	1,2	2,2

An image placed on the screen can be identified by location in one of two ways:

- The image top-left coordinates and bottom-right coordinates.
- The image top-left coordinates and a width and a height

Here are examples of both types of identifiers:

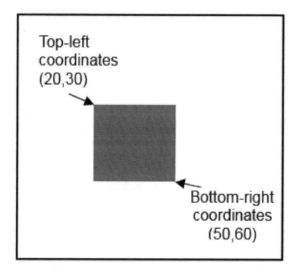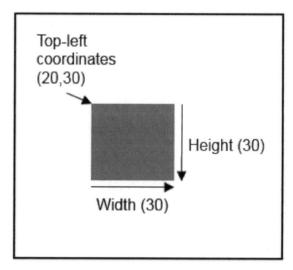

The image on the left shows a block on the screen with its upper-left coordinate pair (point) and its bottom-right coordinate pair (point). With these two pieces of information, you can figure out the width and height of the square with a little simple mathematics:

- The square's width = the bottom-right X coordinate – the upper-left X coordinate.
- The square's height = the bottom-right Y coordinate – the upper-left Y coordinate.

In this example the square's width = 50-20, or 30 pixels and the square's height = 60 – 30, or 30 pixels.

The image on the right shows the same block; although this time we have specified the upper-left point and the width and height of the square. With this information, we can again use some simple math to determine the bottom-right point:

- The square's bottom-right X coordinate = the upper-left X coordinate + the square's width.
- The square's bottom-right Y coordinate = the upper-left Y coordinate + the square's height.

So, in this example the bottom-right X coordinate = 20+30, or 50 and the bottom right Y coordinate = 30+30, or 60. The final bottom-right coordinate pair is (50, 60).

These types of calculations are used fairly often in graphics programming.

Lesson Two: Points

In our last course, we introduced a way to create your own data type with something called a data structure. A structure allows us to group data together into a new, single data type. To define a new data type in Visual Basic, use the **Structure** keyword like this:

```
Public Structure Address
        Dim street As String
        Dim city As String
        Dim state As String
        Dim zip As Integer
End Structure
```

The opening **Structure** statement is followed by your new name for the structure data type, in this case: **Address**. The **Dim** statements inside of the structure define the variables we want to group together in the structure. The **End Structure** statement tells Visual Basic that the data structure has ended.

Once you have defined a new structure, you can create a variable of that new data type:

```
Dim myAddress As Address
```

When we need to assign values to the elements in the **Address** data structure, we use the dot (.) just like using a property from a textbox or other control:

```
myAddress.street = "123 Peachtree Street"
myAddress.city = "Atlanta"
myAddress.state = "GA"
myAddress.zip = 30113
```

We can read these values the same way:

```
MsgBox ("My street is: " & myAddress.street)
```

Structures are a great way to handle the X and Y coordinates of screen pixels, as you'll see next!

Points

The screen on your computer is a good example of a grid or two-dimensional array. Since each pixel is represented by two numbers (X,Y), and we have a large number of pixels on the screen, it would be very convenient to have a data structure that contained both X- and Y-coordinates. That way we could track pixel positions with one named variable. Fortunately, such an object is already defined by Visual Basic -- the **Point**.

The **Point** has two numeric properties: **X** and **Y**. You can use a **Point** to represent either a location (X- and Y-coordinates of a pixel) or a size (width and height, in pixels) of an object. This data type is very useful when you are dealing with graphics because you often track positions of objects on the screen by their pixel coordinates. The upper-left point is often used as the *location* of the object on the screen. The size of a graphic object is also typically defined by both an X (width) value and a Y (height) value.

You can declare an instance of a **Point** just like any other basic data type, and set the X and Y properties just like a standard structure:

```
Dim myPixel As Point
myPixel.X = 100
myPixel.Y = 100
```

We will use the **Point** data type often in our game programs. In addition to pixel coordinates or width and height, you can use a **Point** to represent any two related pieces of numeric data. For instance, you may track an object's speed in the up/down and left/right directions by using a **Point**.

Lesson Three: Drawing Simple Shapes

The Visual Basic Toolbox contains a set of shapes that you can draw on your form. In our last course, we created a "Pong" program that used an **OvalShape** and a **RectangleShape** to create a ball and a paddle for our game. By moving these objects around the screen, we made the ball look like it was bouncing around the screen and the rectangle look like it was hitting the ball as a paddle.

In this lesson, we will take another look at these simple shapes and how they can be moved around a screen. To begin, open the Visual Basic 2010 Express IDE and create a new project called "Shape Test".

Change the Name and Text of "Form1" by clicking on the form and then finding the **(Name)** and **Text** properties in the Property Sheet. Change the **(Name)** property to "ShapeTest" and the **Text** property to "Testing Shapes".

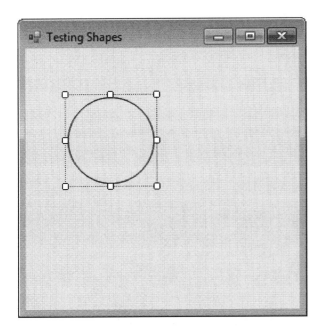

If you look in your Toolbox under the heading "Visual Basic Power Packs", you will see three shapes: **LineShape**, **OvalShape** and **RectangleShape**. Go ahead and draw an **OvalShape** on your form. Your form should look like the example to the left.

Now take a look at the property sheet for this control. There are two important properties for an **OvalShape**: the **Location** and the **Size**. The **Location** is made up of two coordinates: an X and a Y that represent the upper left corner of the circle shape. Since circles have no corners, Visual Basic draws a dotted square around the circle to indicate where the top left point is on your shape.

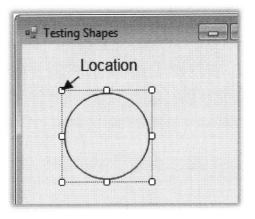

We can use the **Location** property to easily move the shape around the screen. By changing the X coordinate, the circle will move left or right. By changing the Y coordinate, the circle will move either up or down. To see this in action, find the **Location** property in the Property Sheet:

If you click on the arrow to the left of **Location**, the property will expand and show the X and Y coordinates separately:

Location	44, 49
X	44
Y	49

Your coordinates will probably be different than those shown above – that's ok! Now change the X coordinate to move the circle left or right. If you enter a value that is less than the current value, the circle will move left. If you enter a value that is more than the current value, the circle will move to the right. Try both: enter a number in the X column that is less than the current value and hit enter and then try one that is more and hit enter. When you hit enter after changing the number, you will see the circle move on the screen.

Try the same thing with the Y coordinate: enter a number in the Y column that is less than the current value and hit enter and then try one that is more and hit enter. When you enter a number that is less, the circle will move up and when you enter a number that is more, the circle will move down. Notice that larger Y values represent positions further down on the screen!

In the last course, the Pong program used these location properties to make it look like a ball was bouncing around the screen.

The **Size** property is also made up of two values: a width and a height that represent the width and height of the oval. If the height and width are the same, the shape will be a circle. If the height and width are different, the shape will look more like an oval. You can make the shape look like it is growing or shrinking by simply increasing or decreasing the width and height values of the **Size** property. Take a look at the **Size** property and change the values like you changed the **Location** values. Did you see your oval change size?

Next let's add a **RectangleShape** control to our form. Just draw the shape anywhere on your form, which should now look something like this:

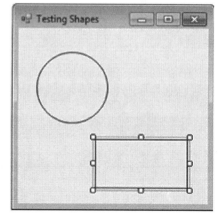

If you look at the property sheet for this control, you will see that it also has the **Location** and **Size** properties. They work the same for the **RectangleShape** as they did in the **OvalShape**. The **Location** property is the X and Y coordinates for the upper-left of the rectangle and the **Size** property has the height and width of the rectangle.

Go ahead and change these values like we did to the **OvalShape**. See if you can move the rectangle left and right and up and down. Now see if you can make it bigger or smaller. Can you make it look like a square by changing the height and width?

The last shape in our toolbox is the **LineShape**. The **LineShape** has a slightly different set of properties than the **OvalShape** or **RectangleShape**. Instead of the **Location** and **Size** properties, the **LineShape** has two sets of coordinates: **X1** and **Y1** and **X2** and **Y2**. These are the two endpoints of the line.

Go ahead and add a **LineShape** to your form.

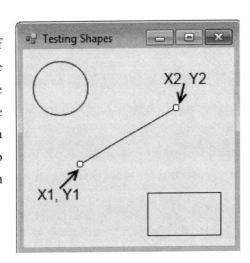

Now you can play with the numbers for **X1**, **Y1** and **X2**, **Y2**. If you change the value of **X1**, the first point of the line will move left and right. If you change the value of **Y1**, the first point of the line will move up and down. If you change the value of **X2**, the second point of the line will move left and right, and if you change the value of **Y2**, the second point of the line will move up and down. Can you make the line go straight up and down? Can you make it go straight from side to side?

Changing these properties in the design window is interesting, but to really animate shapes, you need to be able to change the properties while your program is running. Even better, we can make these shapes move at a certain speed, which really makes them look like they are moving on their own. To animate shapes on the screen we will use the Timer control, which calls an event handler function at regular intervals. Within the event handler function we can programmatically adjust these property values.

In the activity for this chapter, we will be bouncing a line shape around the screen. In order to know when to make our line shape "bounce" we need to know where the top, bottom and sides of the form are when our program is running. To do this, we will use two form properties: **Me.ClientSize.Height** and **Me.ClientSize.Width**. These properties will give us the usable sizes of the height and width of our form.

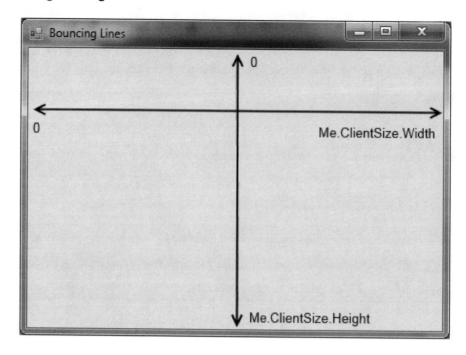

These two form properties will be used often in our games in this course!

We know that we will need to bounce our lines when the X part of our **Location** property is either less than or equal to 0 (we have hit the left side of the screen) or greater than or equal to **Me.ClientSize.Width** (we have hit the right side of the screen). We will also bounce the line when the Y part of our **Location** property is either less than or equal to 0 (we have hit the top of the screen) or greater than or equal to **Me.ClientSize.Height** (we have hit the bottom of our screen).

Chapter Review

- Computer screens are made of individual dots called pixels.
- The resolution of a screen is the number of pixels across by the number of pixels down that the screen can display.
- Pixels on the screen are commonly identified by a coordinate pair, or a point on the screen.
- Each coordinate pair has an X value (left to right) and a Y value (top to bottom).
- Images are located on the screen using the coordinate pair of the upper-leftmost part.
- A data structure is a way to create your own data type.
- A data structure can group variables, arrays and methods together into one group.
- A **Point** is a useful pre-defined object that has two members: **X** and **Y**.
- Line, rectangle, and oval shapes on your form can be moved and resized by adjusting values in the control's Property Sheet.
- You can find the boundaries of your form screen by reading the **Me.ClientSize.Width** and **Me.ClientSize.Height** properties.

Your Turn! Part One: Bouncing Lines

In this activity you will create a program that will bounce a line around the screen.

The starter project for this activity can be found in your "**KidCoder\Game Programming\Activity Starters\Bouncing Line**" directory. The name of the solution for this chapter is "**Bouncing Line.sln**". Go ahead and run the Visual Basic 2010 Express software and open this solution.

The starter project contains the following elements:

- A **LineShape** control, named **BouncingLine**. We will "bounce" this line around the screen.

- A **Timer** control, named **LineTimer**, which will be used to update the line position periodically.

- A **Button** control, named **StartButton**, which will be used to start the line moving on the screen.

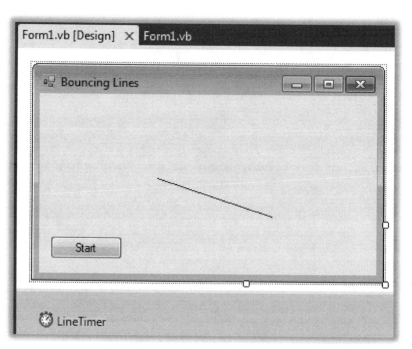

In the code window in the starter project, you will find the following pieces of code already added for you:

- Two **Point** variables, which will be used to track the direction of the two endpoints on our line.

```
Dim point1Direction As Point
Dim point2Direction As Point
```

- An event handler for the **LineTimer Tick** event.
- An event handler for the **StartButton**'s **Click** event.
- A function called **MoveLine()**, in which you will write the code to move the line around the screen. This function will be called from within the **LineTimer_Tick** event.

In order to make a shape move smoothly across the screen we want to make small adjustments to the shape's **Location** property on each timer tick. The sizes of the adjustments in each direction (X and Y) determine how fast the object is moving. The sign (positive or negative) of the adjustment will determine if the object is moving up, down, left, right, or some combination of directions.

You will use the **Point** variables **point1Direction** and **point2Direction** to control the direction of the two points on our line. If **point1Direction**'s X value is negative the point will be moving toward the left, and if it is positive the point will be moving to the right. If **point1Direction**'s Y value is negative the point will be moving upwards; if it is positive, the point will be moving downwards. The same is true for **point2Direction**'s X and Y values.

The size or magnitude of these variables will also determine the speed of the movement. If the value is 1 or -1, the point will move one pixel at a time, which is relatively slow. If the value is 10 or -10, the point will move 10 pixels at a time, which is pretty fast. By changing this value, we can speed up or slow down the movement of our line.

Here are the steps that you need to take to complete this activity:

1. Add the following to the **MoveLine()** function:

   - First, use an **If** statement to check to see if the line's **Y1** position (**BouncingLine.Y1**) is less than or equal to zero. If it is, this means that the first endpoint is above the top of the screen. To bounce the endpoint back down we want to reverse the Y direction, so just multiply **point1Direction**'s Y value by -1 and save this value back into **point1Direction.Y**.

   - Next, use another **If** statement to see if the line's **Y2** position (**BouncingLine.Y2**) is less than or equal to zero. If it is, this means that the second endpoint is above the top of the screen. To bounce the endpoint back down we want to reverse the Y direction, so just multiply **point2Direction**'s Y value by -1 and save this value back into **point2Direction.Y**.

   - Now add two more **If** statements. One **If** will check the line's **Y1** (**BouncingLine.Y1**) value to see if the line has gone past the bottom of the screen. To do this, we will use the value returned by checking the property **Me.ClientSize.Height**. This will tell us the height of the current form (and tell us where the bottom-most point is on the screen).. If **Y1** is greater than or equal to the form height, we will need to bounce the endpoint by multiplying **point1Direction.Y** by -1 and save this value back into **point1Direction.Y**. The second **If** statement will do the same check for the line's **Y2** (**BouncingLine.Y2**) value, bouncing that endpoint by multiplying **point2Direction.Y** by -1 and save this value back into **point2Direction.Y**.

   - You next need to check to see if the line has hit the left or right side of the screen. You will use the X coordinates for these tests. First, use an **If** statement to check the left side by seeing if

BouncingLine.X1 is less than or equal to zero. If it is less than or equal to zero, that endpoint on the line has hit the left side of the screen. We will bounce the line by multiplying **point1Direction.X** by -1 and save this value back into **point1Direction.X**. You will use another **If** statement to do the same check for the line's **X2** (**BouncingLine.X2**) value, bouncing that endpoint by multiplying **point2Direction.X** by -1 and save this value back into **point2Direction.X**.

- Now you will check to see if the line has hit the right side of the screen. To do this, we will a use the value returned by checking the property **Me.ClientSize.Width**. This will tell us the width of the current form (and tell us where the rightmost point is on the screen). You will add two more **If** statements: If **BouncingLine.X1** is greater than or equal to **Me.ClientSize.Width**, we will need to bounce the line by multiplying **point1Direction.X** by -1 and save this value back into **point1Direction.X**. If **BouncingLine.X2** is greater than or equal to **Me.ClientSize.Width**, you need to bounce the line by multiplying **point2Direction.X** by -1 and save this value back into **point2Direction.X**.

- At the end of this step, you should have four **If** statements for the Y values and four **If** statements for the X values.

- Finally, now that you have adjusted both endpoint directions if necessary, you will move your line by updating the position of each endpoint on the screen. You can add the current direction X or Y value to the corresponding X or Y position of each endpoint, like this:

  o Set **BouncingLine.X1** equal to **point1Direction.X + BouncingLine.X1**
  o Set **BouncingLine.Y1** equal to **point1Direction.Y + BouncingLine.Y1**
  o Set **BouncingLine.X2** equal to **point2Direction.X + BouncingLine.X2**
  o Set **BouncingLine.Y2** equal to **point2Direction.Y + BouncingLine.Y2**

2. You will need to call your **MoveLine()** function every time your Timer fires. From within the Timer's **Tick** event, just add a call to the **MoveLine()** function.

3. In the **StartButton_Click** event, you can initialize the X and Y directions of the **point1Direction** and **point2Direction** variables. Set each of the X and Y values of these variables to the value 2.

4. Now you will need to start the Timer whenever the user clicks on the **StartButton**. Under the initialization of the point variables, add a call to **LineTimer.Start()**.

Alright! Run your program and hit the "Start" button. You should see the line move and bounce around the screen! You can try different values for the initial X and Y directions of each endpoint (both positive and negative values, and different numbers in different directions). Your line should start out in a different direction and speed when you change these values!

Your Turn! Part Two: Lines of Color

In this activity, you will add some color to the Bouncing Lines program that you created in the first activity. Go ahead run Visual Basic 2010 Express and open the **Bouncing Lines** project that you finished last time.

This activity will use a Visual Basic data type called **Color**. Colors are defined by the keyword **Color** and a property which defines which color you want to use. Here are examples of several available colors:

```
Color.Blue
Color.Red
Color.Black
```

In the Visual Basic code window, whenever you type in **Color** and then type a period ".", you will see a list of available colors.

Review of Arrays

This program uses an *array* of data, which we discussed in our *KidCoder*[TM]*: Windows Programming* course. Arrays make using groups of one data type very simple. You can create an array of any data type. You can have an array of integers, strings, or other data types. A typical array is declared like this:

```
Dim studentGrade(9) As Integer
```

This will create an array or group of 10 integers. The name of our array is **studentGrade**. Each of the variables in an array is called an *element* and each element can be accessed by a number called an *index*.

 One of the most frequent errors when using arrays is to forget that they are zero-based. The first element of an array is always index 0, NOT index 1!

Each element in the array is named by its index value in parentheses. So to set the first element and last elements in the array, we could use the following code:

```
studentGrade(0) = 95
studentGrade(9) = 100
```

For more information on arrays, please see Chapter 12 in our second edition *KidCoder™: Windows Programming* course.

Back to the Bouncing Lines!

To add colored lines to your Bouncing Lines program, you should do the following:

- At the top of the form add an array named **colorArray** of length 4 with the data type **Color**.

```
Dim colorArray(3) As Color
```

- At the top of the form, add an **Integer** variable **currentColor** that will hold the currently used index of the **colorArray**.
- In the Start Button's **Click** event, add the following:

  o Initialize the **colorArray** with some colors. Make sure you put a value into each element (0, 1, 2, and 3) of the array. You can choose any colors that you would like to use. Example:

```
colorArray(0) = Color.Blue
```

  o Set the **currentColor** index of the color array to 0 (the first color in the array).
  o Set the **BouncingLine**'s **BorderColor** property to the color defined in the array for the current index:

```
BouncingLine.BorderColor = colorArray(currentColor)
```

- To change the color every time the line bounces, create a new function called **ChangeColor**().

```
Private Sub ChangeColor()
End Sub
```

Within the **ChangeColor**() function, you should:

  o Check the **currentColor** index value. If it is less than 3, add 1 to the value. Otherwise, set the value to 0.
  o Set the line's **BorderColor** property to the new current color element:

```
BouncingLine.BorderColor = colorArray(currentColor)
```

- Finally, add the following to the **MoveLine()** function:

  o Add a Boolean variable **isBounced** to the top of the **MoveLine()** function and set the default value to **False**.

  o Now you need to set the **isBounced** value to **True** whenever the line is bounced. In each of your **If** statements, where you have reversed any line's X1, Y1, X2 or Y2 values (multiplying by -1), add another line which sets **isBounced** = **True**.

  o At the bottom of the **MoveLine()** function, check to see if the **isBounced** flag is set to **True**. If it is, call the **ChangeColor()** function.

 **That's it! Try out your program and watch the line change colors every time it bounces on the screen!**

Chapter Four: User Input

In this chapter we will learn about the major ways a user can interact with your game. First we describe the Visual Basic events generated when the user moves or clicks the mouse. Then we will talk about how user key-presses on the keyboard are translated into events that you can handle in your code.

Lesson One: Mouse Events

Your games will likely need to respond to mouse button clicks. There are actually three different events generated when a user clicks a mouse button. You may choose to handle one or more of these events depending on the needs of the game program.

MouseDown	The **MouseDown** event happens whenever a user pushes down on any of the mouse's buttons. This event is useful whenever you want to use "drag" functionality in your program. Dragging the mouse is when you click down in one area of a screen, hold the mouse button down while you move the mouse to another area on the screen, and then release the mouse button.
MouseUp	The **MouseUp** event happens whenever the user lets go of a mouse button. Obviously, this will come after a **MouseDown** event for that button! If you are using the mouse to drag items around the screen, the **MouseUp** event will tell you where the user was when they let go of the item they were moving.
MouseClick	The third click event is the **MouseClick** event. This event fires after the user presses down and then releases the mouse button. This event is used when you just want to know that the mouse was clicked on a certain spot, but are not interested in tracking individual mouse down/up events for "drag" processing.

The event handling functions for all of these events have the exact same parameters. The most important parameter for these events is "**e**". The "**e**" parameter (short for "event arguments") contains all the information about the mouse's current position, which button was clicked, etc. This information allows you to perform actions based on which button was clicked and where the mouse cursor is located on the screen.

Here is a list of some of the information that the "e" parameter contains:

- **e.X**: the current X-coordinate of the mouse pointer
- **e.Y**: the current Y-coordinate of the mouse pointer
- **e.Button**: the current mouse button pressed or clicked

Your mouse event handler subroutine will read this parameter information to process a user's mouse clicks. You may take different actions for the left or right button. You can also use the X and Y-coordinates to determine where the user clicked within the form.

 **A single click of a mouse button will fire off three different events! Your program will receive a MouseDown, MouseUp and MouseClick event for every mouse click! It's up to you whether or not you handle each event.**

Mouse Event Handlers

To create a mouse event handler in your program, you use the drop-down boxes at the top of the code window, just like creating event handlers for any other form component.

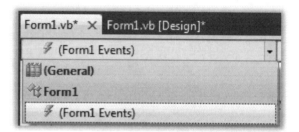

On the left combo box, pick the line called "(Form1 Events)". The actual text will contain the name of your form instead of "Form1". When you pick the Events line on the left, the right combo box will show all of the events that are available for the form itself.

There are a large number of events available for the form, listed alphabetically. Scroll down until you find the "Mouse" events...including those we have been discussing: **MouseClick**, **MouseDown**, and **MouseUp**.

If we were to choose the **MouseClick** event from the list, the code window would automatically create an event handler for this event:

```
Private Sub Form1_MouseClick(ByVal sender As Object, _
                         ByVal e As System.Windows.Forms.MouseEventsArgs)
    End Sub
```

Now this event handler function will be called each time the user clicks the mouse on our form! We can add some code to this function that shows the interesting coordinate and button parameters of the mouse click.

```
Private Sub Form1_MouseClick(ByVal sender As Object, _
                    ByVal e As System.Windows.Forms.MouseEventsArgs)


    If e.Button = MouseButtons.Left Then
        MsgBox("You pressed the left button")


    Else If e.Button = MouseButtons.Right Then
        MsgBox("You pressed the right button")
    End If


    MsgBox("The mouse is located at: X: " & e.X & " Y: " & e.Y)


End Sub
```

The first **MsgBox** statement will use the **e.Button** parameter to see which mouse button was clicked. The most common values you might find in e.**Button** are:

- **MouseButton.Left**
- **MouseButton.Middle**
- **MouseButton.Right**.

If you click the left mouse button, then e.**Button** would equal **MouseButton.Left**, and the resulting message box from the above code would say "You pressed the left button".

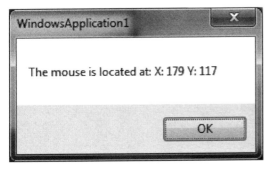

The second **MsgBox** statement in our sample code will use the **e.X** and **e.Y** parameters, which show us the X and Y coordinates of the mouse cursor when the button was clicked. The sample to the left shows that our mouse cursor was located at X=179 and Y=117 when the mouse button was clicked.

These same "e" properties are available to all of the different mouse event handler functions.

Other Mouse Events

In addition to the basic three **MouseUp/MouseDown/MouseClick** events, we will describe two other useful events you may choose to handle in your game.

MouseDoubleClick	The **MouseDoubleClick** event is fired whenever the user clicks the mouse twice very quickly. How quickly? That actually depends on the user's Windows setting. In the control panel, there is a mouse icon where you can set things like the double-click speed of your mouse. The **MouseDoubleClick** event is useful when you want to tell the difference between a user just clicking once on the screen and a user double-clicking on the same spot. For example, in many Windows desktops a single click will highlight an icon, while a double-click will start the icon's application.
MouseMove	The **MouseMove** event will fire every time the mouse moves on the screen. In a typical Windows application where the user is making use of the mouse, this event may fire many times per second! The **MouseMove** event is useful when you need to track where the user is dragging an item on the screen (like when a user is "drawing" on the screen). This event is also useful when you need to move an object on the screen with the mouse movement. We used this functionality in the Pong game in the last course. The Pong paddle was moved back and forth on the screen by tracking mouse movement and setting the paddle's current position according to the mouse's horizontal (X) position.

The event handling functions for both of these events have the exact same parameters as the **MouseDown**, **MouseUp**, and **MouseClick** events. **MouseDoubleClick** and **MouseMove** have an "e" parameter with the same **Button**, **X** and **Y** properties as we discussed for the first three events.

Mouse Cursors

While we are talking about the mouse, it is also fun to learn how to change the mouse pointer (icon) that is displayed to the user! In Visual Basic, these pointers are called "cursors". In most cases the user will see arrow pointer or the hourglass icon. The arrow is just the default cursor for Windows when the program is ready to receive mouse input. The hourglass cursor is universally understood to mean "wait" while the program is busy doing something.

You can easily change the current mouse cursor in your program. The **Cursor** object represents the program's mouse cursor and the **Current** property determines the current cursor's icon. The "Cursors" object contains a set of pre-defined cursors that may be assigned to the Cursor.**Current** property to change the visible mouse icon. For example:

```
Cursor.Current = Cursors.WaitCursor
```

This code will change the current mouse cursor to the hourglass icon. This is extremely useful when you are performing some action in the program and you need the user to wait until you are done. This keeps the user from clicking on the form until you are ready for them to do so.

There are many different cursors that you can use in your program. As soon as you type in the `Cursor.Current =` in your program, Visual Basic will pop-up a list box with over two dozen available built-in cursors. Some example built-in cursors include:

Cursor Type	Icon	Description
Cursors.**Arrow**		The default arrow icon is used to show the program is ready to receive user input.
Cursors.**Help**		The question mark is typically used to show that help is available.
Cursors.**IBeam**		The large capital "i" (I) is used to show that the focus is on a textbox.
Cursors.**SizeNS**		The double "North-South" arrow indicates the object under the mouse can be stretched vertically.

In most cases the operating system will automatically switch between the different types of cursors according to what the user is doing on the screen -- no extra processing is required by your program. However, should you wish to do something special with the mouse icons the **Cursor** class will let you do it!

Lesson Two: Keyboard Events

In this lesson, we will discuss keyboard events. Often a computer game cannot be played strictly with the mouse. Many games require the user to enter information or control objects with the keyboard.

Keyboard events are similar to mouse events as there are three different events that can be handled for each key pressed. You may use one or more of these events depending on the needs of your program.

KeyPress	The **KeyPress** event is fired whenever a user presses and releases a key on the keyboard (similar to the **MouseClick** event). However, this event will only be generated by the character keys on the keyboard. If the user presses "a", "p", "x", etc., the **KeyPress** event will occur. If the user presses the arrow keys, the spacebar, or the TAB key, this event will not occur. Do not use this event if you are trying to capture one of the non-character keys!
KeyDown	The **KeyDown** event is fired every time a user presses down on a key. Unlike the **KeyPress** event, this event will fire for every key on the keyboard, including the non-character keys! This event is useful for tracking when the user is holding down any non-character key such as the spacebar or the shift key.
KeyUp	The **KeyUp** event is fired every time a user lets go of a key that had been pressed down. Just like the **KeyDown** event, this event will fire for every key on the keyboard, including the non-character keys. If the user is holding down the spacebar to fire at an opponent, for example, then the **KeyUp** event would tell you that the user is no longer holding down that key and you can stop firing.

 **The Key Press event will only fire if the user has pressed a character key on the keyboard. The character keys are the keys that create a readable character. The un-readable characters, like the TAB key and the arrow keys are not character keys and will not cause a Key Press event!**

Just like mouse events, these key event handlers all have an "e" parameter. However, the properties of the "e" parameter are different for the **KeyPress** event and the **KeyDown** and **KeyUp** events.

Key Press Event Handlers

The **KeyPress** event handler is added to your program the same way that we added the Mouse event handlers. We first want to choose the item "Form1 Events" from the left combo box above the code window. Then the second combo box will automatically display all of the events for the form, including the key events.

⚡ KeyDown
⚡ KeyPress
⚡ KeyUp

If we were to choose the **KeyPress** event, the code window would automatically get an event handler:

```
        Private Sub Form1_KeyPress(ByVal sender As Object, _
                            ByVal e As System.Windows.Forms.KeyPressEventArgs)
        End Sub
```

The "e" parameter for the **KeyPress** event contains the **KeyChar** property, which holds the character value of the key that was pressed on the keyboard. You can read and store that value in order to do something useful later, or you can take some immediate action based on the key pressed.

It's important to note that the value of the key stored in **KeyChar** is case-sensitive. This means Visual Basic will distinguish between a lower-case "f" and an upper-case "F", treating them as two different characters!

This event handler function will be called each time the user presses a character key on our form. Now let's add some code to the function to show how to use the **e.KeyChar** parameter:

```
        Private Sub Form1_KeyPress(ByVal sender As Object, _
                            ByVal e As System.Windows.Forms.KeyPressEventsArgs)
            MsgBox("You pressed the letter: " & e.KeyChar)
        End Sub
```

The **MsgBox** statement reads the e.**KeyChar** parameter to see which key was pressed. Assuming you pressed the "b" key, this message box would display:

KeyDown and KeyUp Event Handlers

The **KeyDown** and **KeyUp** events have different properties than the **KeyPress** event. Here is a list of some of the properties that the "e" parameter contains for these events:

e.Alt, e.Control, e.Shift (Boolean properties)	If any of these Boolean properties are **True**, then that key has been pressed. Zero, one, or more may be **True** at the same time if multiple keys are being pressed!
e.KeyCode	This property contains a value of the key that was pressed. Key codes are pre-defined properties of the **Keys** object -- one for each key on the keyboard. For example, **Keys.A** represents the "A" key and **Keys.F** represents the "F" key.

Notice that the e.**KeyCode** property for the **KeyDown** and **KeyUp** events is NOT the same as the e.**KeyChar** property for the **KeyPress** event. The e.**KeyCode** parameter does not contain a character like "g", but rather a data value that represents the physical key on the keyboard that was pressed. The **Keys** object allows us to identify keys like the **Keys.Enter** key, the **Keys.Tab** key and the **Keys.Space** key.

You add the **KeyUp** and **KeyDown** event handler functions to your code using the same way that we added the **KeyPress** event handler -- using the drop-down boxes at the top of the code window.

First you want to choose the item "Form1 Events". Then, the second combo box will automatically display all of the events for the form, including the **KeyUp** and **KeyDown** events.

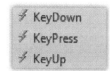

If we were to choose the **KeyDown** event from the list, the following event handler function would automatically be created:

```
Private Sub Form1_KeyDown(ByVal sender As Object, _
                    ByVal e As System.Windows.Forms.KeyEventArgs)
End Sub
```

This event handler function will be called each time the user presses a **KeyDown** on our form! Now we can add some code to this function showing how to use the parameters.

```
Private Sub Form1_KeyDown(ByVal sender As Object, _
                    ByVal e As System.Windows.Forms.KeyEventsArgs)
    MsgBox("You pressed the key: " & e.KeyCode.ToString())
End Sub
```

The **MsgBox** statement will use the e.**KeyCode** parameter to see which keyboard key is pressed down. The **ToString()** method on the **KeyCode** object will just format the key name nicely for our **MsgBox**. The resulting message box would look like this if you pressed the TAB key:

The **KeyUp** event handler is identical to the **KeyDown** handler. The only difference, as you have already guessed, is when the two events are called. The **KeyDown** event handler is called whenever the key is pushed down; the **KeyUp** is called when it is let up again.

Lesson Three: The Select Statement

In this lesson we will learn about the **Select** statement, which is another version of the **If-Else** statement. The **If-Else** statement is great when you only have a few possible conditions to check. But, when you start adding more and more possible values, the **If-Else** statement can become a little complicated. For example, let's say you need to know whether or not the user has pressed the "A" key. You create a **KeyPress** event handler and write an **If-Else** statement to check to see if they have pressed that key:

```
If e.KeyChar = "A" Then
      'do something here
End If
```

That looks pretty simple and straightforward. Now let's say we also need to know if they have pressed the "S", "D" or "G" keys:

```
If e.KeyChar = "A" Then
            'do something here
Else If e.KeyChar = "S" Then
            'do something else here
Else If e.KeyChar = "D" Then
            'do something else here
Else If e.KeyChar = "G" Then
            'do something else here
End If
```

Now that looks a little messy and more complicated. This is true for most big **If** statements. They are easy to read when you are testing one or two conditions. If you are testing more than two conditions, they begin to look cluttered.

The **Select** statement allows you to test one variable or expression for many different values.

```
Select Case <expression>
    Case <first value to check>
            <statement(s) to execute if expression equals first value>
    Case <second value to check>
            <statement(s) to execute if expression equals second value>
    Case Else
            <statement(s) to execute if expression equals none of above>
End Select
```

This statement starts with the keywords **Select Case** followed by a variable or an expression. Each **Case** statement below then gives one possible "answer" for the **Select** expression. If the expression equals that **Case** answer, then the statements within the **Case** will be executed.

A **Select** statement can contain as many **Cases** as you need. The final **Case Else** is a catch-all condition, which will be executed if no other **Case** value equaled the **Select** expression. You do not have to include a **Case Else** in your **Select** statements but it is usually good programming practice to set some default logic in case your expression doesn't match any of the expected values. The **Select** syntax closed out with the final **End Select** line.

Now, let's re-write our **If-Else** example code above using a **Select** statement:

```
Select Case e.KeyChar
    Case "A"
        'do something when key = A
    Case "S"
        'do something when key = S
    Case "D"
        'do something when key = D
    Case "G"
        'do something when key = G
    Case Else
        'do something when key is any other value
End Select
```

Using a **Select** statement to test many values is usually cleaner and easier to read than many **If-Else** statements!

You can also use the **Select** statement to easily find out where a variable or expression falls within a range of numbers. For example, let's say we have a numeric variable called **studentGrade**. We want to print out a different message based on the value in this variable. Here is what that code might look like if we used an **If-Else** statement:

```
If (studentGrade = 100) Then
    MsgBox("Perfect Score!")

Else If (studentGrade >= 90 And studentGrade < 100) Then
    MsgBox("Great job! You get an A!")

Else If (studentGrade >= 80 And studentGrade < 90) Then
    MsgBox("Good job. You get a B.")
```

```
    Else If (studentGrade >= 70 And studentGrade < 80) Then
        MsgBox("Not bad. You get a C.")


    Else If (studentGrade >= 60 And studentGrade < 70) Then
        MsgBox("Needs improvement. You get a D.")
    Else
        MsgBox("Oh dear. You get an F!")
    End If
```

Notice how we have to join two different expressions with the keyword **And** in order to test to see if the grade falls within a certain range. The **Select** statement allows you to test a range of numbers using the **To** keyword in the **Case** statement.

```
    Select Case studentGrade
        Case 100
            MsgBox("Perfect Score!")


        Case 90 To 99
            MsgBox("Great job! You get an A!")


        Case 80 To 89
            MsgBox("Good job! You get a B.")


        Case 70 To 79
            MsgBox("Not bad. You get a C.")


        Case 60 To 69
            MsgBox("Needs improvement. You get a D.")


        Case Else
            MsgBox("Oh dear. You get an F!")
    End Select
```

You can see how much simpler this is to read when compared to the **If-Else** statement. If the value of **studentGrade** is between the numbers 90 and 99, the second case statement will execute, if the value is between 80 and 89, the third case statement will execute and so on.

We will use the **Select** statement for several of our games in this course. For this chapter's activity, you will use the **Select** statement to check and see what key the user has pressed on the keyboard.

Chapter Review

- When the user clicks the mouse, three different events will fire: the **MouseDown**, the **MouseClick** and the **MouseUp** events.

- Each mouse event has a parameter "**e**", which will tell you which button was clicked, and where the mouse was on the screen.

- The mouse also has a **DoubleClick** event, which fires when the user double-clicks one of the mouse buttons.

- The **MouseMove** event will occur every time the mouse moves on the screen.

- When the user hits any key on the keyboard, two different events will fire: the **KeyDown**, and the **KeyUp**.

- If the user has hit a character key, the **KeyPress** event will also fire.

- The key events have a parameter "**e**", which will tell you what key has been hit.

- The mouse pointer on the screen is called a **Cursor** in Visual Basic.

- The cursor can be changed by setting the Cursor.**Current** property.

- The **Select** statement allows you to test one variable or expression for many different values.

- The **Select** statement can be cleaner and simpler to write than a group of **If-Else** statements.

Your Turn! Part One - Dancing Squares

In this activity, you will create a program that responds to a user's key presses and mouse movements.

The starter project for this activity can be found in your "**KidCoder\Game Programming\Activity Starters\Dancing Shapes**" directory. The name of the solution for this chapter is "**Dancing Shapes.sln**". Go ahead and start up Visual Basic 2010 Express and open this solution.

This program will display square and circle shapes on the screen. In Part One of this activity, we want the user to move, resize, and change the color of the square shape by pressing certain keys on the keyboard. In Part Two you will use the mouse to control the circle.

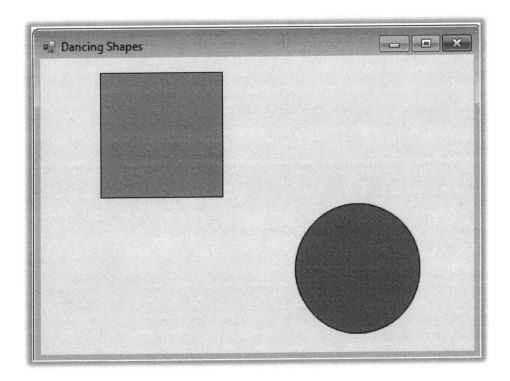

The starter project contains the following things already added for you:

- A **RectangleShape** control named **DancingSquare**.

- An array that holds 4 different colors for the square.

```
Dim squareColorArray() As Color = {Color.Blue, Color.Red, _
                                   Color.Green, Color.Yellow}
```

- An index variable **currentSquareColor** which will be the index into the **squareColorArray**.

```
Dim currentSquareColor As Integer = 0
```

- You will also have some elements that we will use in Part Two of this activity:

    o An **OvalShape** control named **DancingCircle**.
    o An array that will hold 4 different colors for the circle:

```
Dim circleColorArray() As Color = {Color.Red, Color.Aqua, _
                                   Color.Chocolate, Color.Fuchsia}
```

    o An index variable **currentCircleColor** which will be the index into the **circleColorArray**.

```
Dim currentCircleColor As Integer = 0
```

Here are the steps that you will need to do on your own:

- Find or create the event handler for the **KeyPress** event.
- Inside the event handler, use a **Select** statement to check which key the user has pressed.

```
Select Case e.KeyChar
```

- Create a **Case** for each of the following four possible key presses:
    o Pressing the "**w**" key will move the square shape up towards the top of the screen. This means that you will need to subtract 1 from the **DancingSquare.Top** property.
    o Pressing the "**a**" key will move the square shape to the left on the screen. This means that you will need to subtract 1 from the **DancingSquare.Left** property.
    o Pressing the "**x**" key will move the square down towards the bottom of the screen. This means that you will need to add 1 to the **DancingSquare.Top** property.
    o Pressing the "**d**" key will move the square to the right on the screen. This means that you will need to add 1 to the **DancingSquare.Left** property.

- Next, find or create the event handler for the **KeyDown** event.
- Inside the event handler, use a select statement to check which key the user has pressed.

```
Select Case e.KeyCode
```

- Create a **Case** for each of the following three possible key presses:
  - o Pressing the **Home** key will make the square larger. This means that you will need to add 1 to both the **Height** and **Width** of the `DancingSquare`.
  - o Pressing the **End** key will make the square smaller. This means that you will need to subtract 1 from the **Height** and **Width** of the `DancingSquare`.
  - o Pressing the **F5** key will change the color of the square. You will need to check the current value of the `currentSquareColor` variable. If it is less than 3, add 1 to this value. If it is 3 or above, set it equal to 0. Then you will need to set the **DancingSquare.FillColor** equal to the color in the `squareColorArray` using the `currentSquareColor` index.

Since the **KeyDown** event uses a **KeyCode** to identify the key that was pressed, you will use the values **Keys.Home**, **Keys.End**, and **Keys.F5** in your **Case** statements.

Now run your program and confirm that the square moves, grows, shrinks, and changes color when you press the right keys!

Your Turn! Part Two - Dancing Circles

In this activity, you will add some Mouse Events to your Dancing Shapes program to control the circle shape. When the left mouse button is clicked, the circle should get larger. When the right mouse button is clicked, the circle should get smaller. When you double-click the circle color should change. Finally, the circle location should follow the mouse cursor on the screen!

To make all of these circle controls work, here's what you need to do:

- Add the following logic to the **MouseClick** event handler:

  o If the button that was clicked was the Left mouse button:

```
If e.Button = MouseButtons.Left Then
```

  - Then add 5 to the **Width** and **Height** properties of the **DancingCircle**.

  o If the button that was clicked was the Right mouse button:

```
If e.Button = MouseButtons.Right Then
```

  - Then subtract 5 from the **Width** and **Height** properties of the **DancingCircle**.

- In the **Mouse Double-Click** event handler, check the current value of the **currentCircleColor** variable. If it is less than 3, add 1 to this value. If it is 3 or above, set it equal to 0. Then you will set the **DancingCircle.FillColor** equal to the current color in the **circleColorArray**.

- Finally, in the **MouseMove** event :

  o Set the **DancingCircle.Left** property to **e.X** and the **DancingCircle.Top** property to **e.Y**

 Now run your program and make sure the circle will grow, shrink, change color, and move as you use the mouse!

Chapter Five: Graphics in Visual Basic

In this chapter you will learn how to programmatically create shapes on the screen without going through the toolbox in the form design screen. You will explore how to draw shapes using different colors and fill textures. Finally, we will walk through the creation of a simple painting program to demonstrate use of the graphics commands.

Lesson One: The Graphics Object

In our last chapter we used the shape controls from the toolbox to create shapes on the screen. The shape controls work great when you know what shape you want to draw before the program even starts. But what if you wanted to create some new graphics during your program? In that case you don't know the number and type of shapes to drag onto the form in advance. Instead, we want to use the Visual Basic Graphics object to create new shapes whenever we need.

The **Graphics** object allows you to draw lines, shapes, images and text directly to the screen. This object can be thought of as the paper for your artwork. On this "paper" you will draw all of the visual elements for your games. The Graphics object has many powerful features, allowing you to draw simple or complex scenes in a very easy manner.

 **Most of the games in this course will use the Graphics object. This object can be used to draw shapes, lines and images on the screen. You can then make the shapes move, rotate and interact with other graphics on the screen.**

The first step in using the Graphics object is to "import" the library that contains the object. To do this, we can add the following code to the top of our Visual Basic form *.vb file:

```
Imports System.Drawing
Imports System.Drawing.Drawing2D
```

These two statements simply tell Visual Basic that we will be using the **Graphics** library in our code. You will place these lines above the line "**Public Class** <FormName>" for every game that we create in this course.

Every form in Visual Basic has its own **Graphics** object. This is the object that Visual Basic uses to draw the buttons, textboxes, labels, etc. on the form. Where do we use the **Graphics** object? In the **Paint()** subroutine! **Paint()** will be very important to understand as you write your games!

Paint() is an event handler that is called automatically whenever the screen needs to be redrawn. To create the Paint() function in your code, just use the combo boxes at the top of your form code screen to select the "(Form Events)" on the left, and then "Paint" on the right:

The Paint() event handler function will then be created in your code:

```
Private Sub Form1_Paint(ByVal sender As Object, _
                  ByVal e As System.Windows.Forms.PaintEventArgs) _
                  Handles Me.Paint


    ' all of your drawing code will go in here!


End Sub
```

Now where do we get the **Graphics** object for this form? The "e" parameter holds it! It's usually easiest to declare a **Graphics** variable within the **Paint()** function and then assign **e.Graphics** to it.

```
Dim myGraphics As Graphics = e.Graphics
```

Now we can use the **myGraphics** variable to draw on this form's screen area.

That's it! Now we are ready to draw some graphics to the screen. In the next lesson, we will talk about the different types of drawing that are possible with the **Graphics** object.

Lesson Two: Pens, Brushes, and Shapes

In our last lesson, we learned how to get the **Graphics** object that will act as the paper for our drawings. Like any drawing, we will need to use pens and brushes to create our artwork!

Shapes such as circles or squares can be drawn as outlines only or as filled shapes. You would use a **Pen** to draw an outline, or use a **Brush** to fill in a shape.

Pens

In Visual Basic the **Pen** object is used to draw lines or shapes. A **Pen** is very similar to the pens that you probably have at your desk. These pens can be any color and can draw with thin lines or thick lines.

To create a pen, you declare a variable of type **Pen**. You then create a **Pen** and assign it to the variable by using the **New** keyword. The parameters passed to the **Pen** when calling **New** are the pen's color and width, in pixels. This sample shows how to declare and create a black **Pen** that will draw lines 2 pixels wide:

```
Dim myPen As Pen = New Pen(Color.Black, 2)
```

Brushes

In Visual Basic the **Brush** object is used to fill objects with color or textures (images). Brushes are similar real brushes you might find in your garage. There are different kinds of brushes depending on what sort of color or texture you would like to paint.

Brush Type	Parameters	Sample	Description
SolidBrush	Color		Fill a shape with a single solid color
TextureBrush	Image		Fill a shape with an image loaded from file
HatchBrush	HatchStyle, Color 1, Color 2		Fill a shape with patterns. The **HatchBrush** uses two colors: one as a background and the other as the pattern color. There are different **HatchStyles** that can be used. Some of the more common are: **DashedHorizontal**, which creates a pattern of dashes that display diagonally, **DiagonalBrick**, which creates a brick-like pattern, and **DottedGrid**, which makes a grid-like set of dots.

| LinearGradientBrush | Rectangle, Color 1, Color 2, LinearGradientMode | | Fill a shape with a blend of colors. The **LinearGradientBrush** uses two colors that will be gradually blended together inside a shape. The **LinearGradientMode** determines whether the colors are blended in a vertical, horizontal or diagonal direction. The Rectangle parameter sets the area to fill. |

The following code shows you how to declare and initialize variables of each brush type that produces the sample images shown above:

```
Dim mySolidBrush As SolidBrush = New SolidBrush(Color.Red)

Dim myTextureBrush As TextureBrush = _
        New TextureBrush(Image.FromFile("C:\images\shopping_cart.gif"))

Dim myHashBrush As HatchBrush = _
        New HatchBrush(HatchStyle.DottedGrid, Color.Black, Color.White)

Dim rect1 = New Rectangle(10, 10, 50, 50)
Dim myLinearGradientBrush As LinearGradientBrush = _
        New LinearGradientBrush(rect1, Color.Green, Color.Blue, _
        LinearGradientMode.Vertical)
```

> **STOP** Pens and Brushes are similar items in Visual Basic. Remember that Pens are used for drawing lines and Brushes are used to fill-in shapes.

Now that we have our paper (the **Graphics** object), **Pens**, and **Brushes**, we can start drawing! There are many different shapes that we can draw onto our **Graphics** object.

Drawing Lines

The simplest shape is the line. To draw a line on the screen, we need to know the starting point and ending point for our line, and we need to have a **Pen**. From within the **Paint**() function, here is how we could create a line:

```
Dim myGraphics As Graphics = e.Graphics

Dim myPen As Pen = New Pen(Color.Blue, 2)
Dim startingPoint As Point = New Point(5,5)
Dim endingPoint As Point = New Point(100,100)

myGraphics.DrawLine(myPen, startingPoint, endingPoint)
```

The above code would draw a blue line that starts at point (5, 5) and ends at point (100,100).

You could also list out each X and Y endpoint coordinate in the **DrawLine**() statement instead of giving two **Points**. This call to **DrawLine**() creates an identical line:

```
myGraphics.DrawLine(myPen, 5, 5, 100, 100)
```

Drawing Ellipses

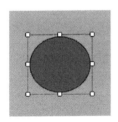 The first **Graphics** function we will talk about draws ellipses. Remember that a circle is just an ellipse where the width and the height are the same! When drawing an ellipse on the screen, you will choose the location and the width and height. For shapes like ellipses that are not rectangular, you can imagine a rectangle drawn tightly around the shape so it's just big enough to include the entire shape (see left example). This imaginary rectangle is called the "bounding rectangle". The location of the ellipse is set by the coordinates of the upper-left corner of the bounding rectangle.

A **Rectangle** is a special Visual Basic data type that holds all of the information about a rectangle. A **Rectangle** has **X** and **Y** properties which represent the upper-left coordinates (location). It also has a **Width** and a **Height**, which give the size of the rectangle. This data type is very useful when you are dealing with graphics on the screen, since most on-screen graphics are defined by a bounding rectangle.

To draw an ellipse we need to make a **Pen**, a **Rectangle**, and then call **Graphics.DrawEllipse**().

```
Dim myPen As New Pen(Color.Red, 2)
Dim myRect As Rectangle = New Rectangle(5,5,50,50)
myGraphics.DrawEllipse(myPen, myRect)
```

The above code draws the outline of an ellipse that starts at location (5, 5) and is 50 pixels wide and 50 pixels high. Since the width and height are the same, we have made a circle!

You can also draw an ellipse by individually listing the X, Y, width, and height values:

```
myGraphics.DrawEllipse(myPen, 5, 5, 50, 50)
```

Again, this only draws the *outline* of an ellipse. To draw a solid-colored ellipse, we would use the **FillEllipse**() function and a brush instead of a pen.

```
Dim mySolidBrush As New SolidBrush(Color.Red)
Dim myRect As Rectangle = New Rectangle(5,5,50,50)
myGraphics.FillEllipse(mySolidBrush, myRect)
```

 This code looks very similar to the **DrawEllipse** function. We still use a **Rectangle** to define our ellipse, but we replace **myPen** with **mySolidBrush** and **DrawEllipse**() with **FillEllipse**(). The result is a solid red circle.

Drawing Rectangles

Another common shape is the rectangle. The **Graphics** object has functions that will draw rectangles, and they look very much like the ellipse functions! Remember too that a square is just a rectangle with equal width and height. To create a rectangle on the screen, we would use the following code:

```
Dim myPen As New Pen(Color.Red, 2)
Dim myRect As Rectangle = New Rectangle(5,5,50,50)
myGraphics.DrawRectangle(myPen, myRect)
```

 This example draws a rectangle starting at point (5,5) with a width and height of 50. Since the height and width are the same, the resulting shape would be a square. As you can see, this code is almost identical to the code we used to create an ellipse.

DrawRectangle() only draws the *outline* of a rectangle. To draw a solid-colored rectangle, we would use the **FillRectangle**() function and a brush instead of a pen.

```
Dim mySolidBrush As New SolidBrush(Color.Red)
Dim myRect As Rectangle = New Rectangle(5,5,50,50)
myGraphics.FillRectangle(mySolidBrush, myRect)
```

This code looks very similar to the **DrawRectangle**() function. We are still using a **Rectangle** to define our shape, but we replace `myPen` with `mySolidBrush` and **DrawRectangle**() with **FillRectangle**(). The result is a solid red square.

Drawing Other Shapes

There are many other shapes that can be drawn besides ellipses and rectangles. We will not walk through all of them, but here is a list of the some other drawing functions on the **Graphics** object:

- **DrawArc**(), **DrawCurve**()
- **DrawPie**(), **FillPie**()
- **DrawPolygon**(), **FillPolygon**()

You can of course use any combination of pens and brushes, fills, textures, images, and gradients to create your own unique graphics!

Invalidation – Forcing the Screen to Redraw

All of the code we have shown so far will be placed directly in your Form's **Paint**() method. The **Paint**() method is responsible for painting everything you see in a form window. Within the **Paint**() method you get the **Graphics** object and can draw your shapes on the form.

However, we need to understand how and why the **Paint**() method will be called in the first place! The function will automatically be called any time Windows knows the screen should be repainted. For instance, **Paint**() will happen when you click away from the screen (maybe to another application) and then click back. Or, this event will also fire if a pop-up window or message box is shown on the screen. Once the message box goes away, the form knows that it needs to re-display.

In game programming you will usually want to force the screen to repaint often, even if the user is not doing anything at the moment. For instance, if a ball is bouncing across the screen, **Paint**() will have to be called many times a second to give the appearance of smooth animation. You can force the **Paint** event to run by calling the **Invalidate**() function. The **Invalidate**() function tells the form that we believe it is time to re-display the screen, and the **Paint** event will fire. To use the **Invalidate**() command, just do this:

```
Invalidate()
```

Pretty simple, right? Yet this is a very useful command. You will most commonly call **Invalidate**() from within your timer Tick method, forcing the screen to repaint at the interval controlled by your timer.

The Invalidate() function is extremely important in game programming. Game screens must be redrawn on the screen to show the motion and interaction of objects on the screen. Invalidate() will force the screen to re-draw after it is called.

Lesson Three: My Paint Program

In this lesson we will build a very simple drawing program.

The complete project for this sample program can be found in your "**\KidCoder\Game Programming\Activity Starters\My Paint**" directory. The name of the solution for this chapter is "**My Paint.sln**". Go ahead and open up Visual Basic 2010 Express and load this solution. Then you can follow along as we explain how the program works. At the end of the chapter you will get a chance to add some drawing options to this program on your own!

Our paint program users will choose a shape to draw from a series of Radio Buttons. A Radio Button is a control that has a label and a small white circle like this:

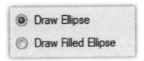

When you click on a Radio Button a black dot will be drawn on the white circle to show that control is selected. If the control has an empty white circle then that button is not selected. Only one radio button can be selected at any one time. We use radio buttons to let the user pick what they want to draw.

Once the user has selected the type of shape, they can click down the left mouse button at the starting point for the shape and "drag" the shape out to the desired size.

The initial form will look like this:

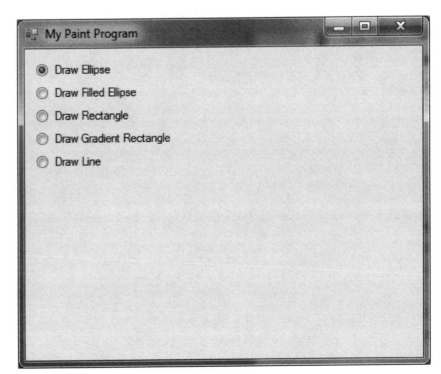

One of these functions will be called depending on which radio button has been selected:

DrawEllipse()	Draws an ellipse outline with a blue pen
DrawFilledEllipse()	Draws a filled ellipse with a solid pink brush
DrawRectangle()	Draws a rectangle outline with a blue pen
DrawGradientRectangle()	Draws a filled rectangle using a gradient brush blending yellow and blue
DrawLine()	Draws a simple line with a blue pen

My Paint Form

The My Paint project contains one **PaintForm** screen with the following controls:

- A radio button named **EllipseRadio** that has the text "Draw Ellipse"
- A radio button named **FilledEllipseRadio** that has the text "Draw Filled Ellipse"
- A radio button named **RectangleRadio** that has the text "Draw Rectangle"
- A radio button named **GradientRectangleRadio** that has the text "Draw Gradient Rectangle"
- A radio button named **LineRadio** that has the text "Draw Line"

The form also declares the following variables

`Dim startingPoint As Point`	This **Point** tracks the starting point for the object to be drawn
`Dim endingPoint As Point`	This **Point** tracks the ending point that determines the object's size
`Dim drawingRect As Rectangle`	This Rectangle combines the **startingPoint** and **endingPoint** to form one of the inputs to the drawing functions.

Mouse Handling Functions

We want the user to be able to click the form to start the shape, and then drag until they reach the size they want. We will use the **MouseDown** event to record the starting point and the **MouseMove** function to set the current ending point.

Here is the **MouseDown** function implementation:

```
Private Sub PaintForm_MouseDown(ByVal sender As Object, _
    ByVal e As System.Windows.Forms.MouseEventArgs) Handles Me.MouseDown
        startingPoint.X = e.X
        startingPoint.Y = e.Y

        drawingRect.X = e.X
        drawingRect.Y = e.Y
    End Sub
```

The **MouseEventArgs** "e" variable passed into this function contains all the information about the location of the mouse when the user clicked a button down. We save the X and Y location of the mouse into the **startingPoint** and also into the **drawingRect**'s **X** and **Y** properties. Now we have captured where the user wants to start drawing the shape!

Now, as the user is dragging the mouse, we want to keep track of the size of the shape and cause the new shape to be redrawn on the screen. We will use the **MouseMove** event to track this size. Here is the **MouseMove** function implementation:

```vb
Private Sub PaintForm_MouseMove(ByVal sender As Object, _
    ByVal e As System.Windows.Forms.MouseEventArgs) Handles Me.MouseMove

        If e.Button <> Windows.Forms.MouseButtons.Left Then
            Exit Sub
        End If

        endingPoint.X = e.X
        endingPoint.Y = e.Y

        drawingRect.Width = endingPoint.X - startingPoint.X
        drawingRect.Height = endingPoint.Y - startingPoint.Y

        Invalidate()
End Sub
```

The first thing we do is check to see if the user is moving the mouse with the left button held down. If not we just exit the function without doing anything.

If they are pressing the left button, we first set the new **endingPoint** from the mouse cursor's current coordinates. To calculate the width and height values, we need to know how far the mouse has traveled from its starting position. We can get this value by subtracting the starting point's **X** value from the current point's **X** value (to get the width) and by subtracting the starting point's **Y** value from the current point's **Y** value (to get the height).

Finally, we call the **Invalidate()** function, which will repaint the screen with our new shape or line.

Paint Function

All drawing to the screen happens within the form's paint function. For this program we will only draw the shape currently chosen by the user, so we will only be drawing one object on the screen at a time.

Here is what we will do in the **Paint** function:

1. Get the Graphics object from the **Paint** parameters and assign to **myGraphics** for our use.

2. Create the pen and brushes that we need to draw our shapes:

    - The pen has a blue color and line width of 1 pixel.
    - The solid brush has a pink color
    - The gradient brush uses entire form as the bounding rectangle, and mixes the colors blue and yellow in a horizontal blend.

```
Dim myPen As Pen = New Pen(Color.Blue, 1)
Dim mySolidBrush As Brush = New SolidBrush(Color.Pink)
Dim myGradientBrush As Brush = New LinearGradientBrush( _
       New Rectangle(0, 0, Me.ClientSize.Width, Me.ClientSize.Height), _
          Color.Blue, Color.Yellow, LinearGradientMode.Horizontal)
```

3. In order to know what shape we are drawing in the **Paint** event, we use a series of **If…ElseIf** statements to check to each of our radio buttons.

4. When the user selects a radio button, the button's **Checked** property is set to **True**. When we find the control where **Checked** = **True**, we then call the right drawing method on **myGraphics**.

```
If EllipseRadio.Checked Then
     myGraphics.DrawEllipse(myPen, drawingRect)
ElseIf FilledEllipseRadio.Checked Then
     myGraphics.FillEllipse(mySolidBrush, drawingRect)
ElseIf RectangleRadio.Checked Then
     myGraphics.DrawRectangle(myPen, drawingRect)
ElseIf GradientRectangleRadio.Checked Then
     myGraphics.FillRectangle(myGradientBrush, drawingRect)
ElseIf LineRadio.Checked Then
     myGraphics.DrawLine(myPen, startingPoint, endingPoint)
End If
```

That's it! With only a few functions we have created a simple painting program. Build and run the program yourself to try it out. You can experiment with different pens, brushes, and shapes.

Chapter Review

- The **Graphics** object is used to draw lines, shapes and images on the screen.

- The **Graphics** object requires the "System.Drawing" and "System.Drawing.Drawing2D" libraries.

- Every Visual Basic form has its own **Graphics** object, which is provided in the form's **Paint** event.

- **Pens** are devices that are used to draw lines or shapes.

- **Pens** can contain just about any color and can draw with thin or thick lines.

- **Brushes** are used to fill objects with color, textures, patterns, or blends of two colors

- The **Graphics** object has many drawing functions to display shapes on the screen.

- In order to force the form to repaint, you need to call the **Invalidate()** function.

Your Turn! Create Your Own Shapes

In this activity, you will give My Paint program the ability to draw a filled rectangle with the solid blue brush and a filled ellipse with the hatched brush.

The starter project for this activity can be found in your "**\KidCoder\Game Programming\Activity Starters\My Paint**" directory. The name of the solution for this chapter is "**My Paint.sln**". Go ahead and open up Visual Basic 2010 Express and load this solution.

Make the following changes to the program:

- Add a radio button named **FilledRectangleRadio** to the form for the solid blue rectangle.
- Add a radio button named **HatchedEllipseRadio** to the form for the hatched, filled ellipse.
- In **Paint()** create a **HatchedBrush** with the **HatchStyle.Cross** style and Red and Green colors:

```
Dim myHatchedBrush = New HatchBrush(HatchStyle.Cross, Color.Red, Color.Green)
```

- In **Paint()**, create a **SolidBrush** variable named **myBlueBrush** with **Color.Blue**.
- In **Paint()**, add two more **Else-If** statements to see if the two new radio buttons are checked.
    - If the **FilledRectangleRadio** radio button is checked, use the **FillRectangle()** function with **myBlueBrush** and the **drawingRect** to draw a filled blue rectangle on the screen.
    - If the **HatchedEllipseRadio** radio button is checked, use the **FillEllipse()** with **myHatchedBrush** and the **drawingRect** to create a filled ellipse with hatched pattern.

When you build and run your program the two new shapes should be available through the radio buttons and should draw correctly on the screen.

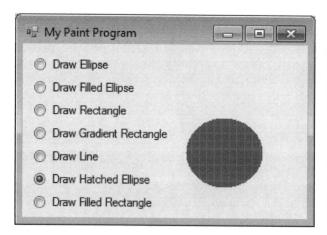

Feel free to experiment! Change the colors and styles of the pens and brushes for the different effects!

Chapter Six: Images and Animation

In this chapter you will learn how to load images into your program and how to animate pictures on the screen.

Lesson One: Animation Concepts

Animation is the art of making still images move. Movies, television programs, and computer programs all display images that appear to move in a lifelike manner on the screen. Are the images on the screen really moving? Nope! The animations are made up of still images flashed past your eyes so fast that your brain blends the images together, giving the illusion of movement. Scientific research tells us that the eye needs to see somewhere between 18 and 24 images per second in order for this illusion to work. Good computer animation will show you a series of images at these speeds or higher.

Flipbooks

In the early 1900's a company called CrackerJack started using a form of art called flipbook animation. Each box of crackerjack candy contained a series of drawings in a tiny book. When the pages of the book were "flipped" or displayed very quickly one-after-another, the image would appear to be in motion. These simple animations were some of the cheapest movies of that time!

 **The original CrackerJack books were very popular and highly prized. What animations did they display? Cartoons? Comics? No, the first CrackerJack books were used to teach dance steps!**

Flipbook animation is still a popular tool for teaching modern animation techniques. Many computer animators will test an animation by first drawing a series of rough images and then flipping the images to see if the end result is give the correct illusion of movement. The same theories of flipbook animation on paper will work for animation in a computer game.

Computer Animation

Like flipbooks, computer animation uses a series of images to show the illusion of motion. You can create simple animations or complex animations, depending on your own skill as an artist. Regardless of your skill, you can create images for your animation by following some simple steps:

1. Decide what the subject and size of your animation will be.
2. Open up your favorite drawing program (Windows Paint is available on most Windows systems)
3. Create a series of images, all of the same size. Each image will be a frame in your animation.
4. Draw the beginning and ending frames first, and then fill in the images in between.
5. Make small changes to your drawing from one image to the next. Too much change makes the image appear to jerk instead of flow across the screen

In addition to these steps, you need to pay attention to what objects really look like when they are moving and interacting with other objects. Take a look at the following set of images:

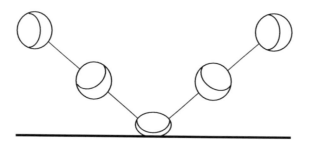

We have added a couple of special touches to make the bouncing ball seem more realistic. First, we added a stripe to the ball and rotated it a bit in each frame, so the ball will appear to spin as it moves. Second, notice that the ball is drawn as almost an oval when it hits the ground. Have you ever noticed that about a bouncing ball? The ball will change shape briefly as it hits the ground. By adding this little change to our animation, it becomes much more life-like.

How many unique images or frames do we have in the above sequence? That's right, only four! The last image in the upper right is identical to the first image, so that last image is really just the first step in the next cycle. You may want to continually animate some object by repeating the same set of images over and over again. For instance, you may have a flag on the screen that should flap continually in the breeze. You can probably create that effect with only a handful of images. Be sure that your last image flows nicely back into your first image so the user doesn't see some sort of jerky restart when the first image is displayed.

If you are not very confident in your artistic skills, here is a technique you can use to still produce a good looking animation. Let's say we wanted to create a 10-image animation of a stick figure being drawn on a blank paper.

- You know what the first image is (#1 - a blank paper) and the last image (#10 - a completed stick figure), so draw those first.
- Take image #10 of the completed stick figure and copy it to image #9. Then erase one of the figure's arms in image #9.
- Take image #9 and copy it to image #8. Then erase one of the figure's legs in image #8.
- Continue this process for images #7 through #2, where image #2 should almost be completely empty.

When this series of images is animated from #1 to #10, it will appear as if the stick figure is being drawn right before your eyes! Knowing your starting point and ending point, and then copying one frame to the next before making your small changes is a great technique for simple animation.

Play around, have some fun! Try creating some frames on paper and flip through them to visualize the results. Flipbook animation is a really easy way to design computer animations.

When you want to provide animations for your own programs, how should you get the image files? One option is to create your own! You can use the Paint program that comes with Windows or any of the many other free or commercial drawing programs available. You can also search online for sources of free or commercial animation files.

Lesson Two: Loading and Displaying Images From Files

In the last lesson, we discussed how to create the images that you will need for a computer animation. Now we will take a look at how to load these images in a program.

Each frame or image in your animation sequence will be represented by a variable in your program. A special data type called, appropriately, **Image**, will represent one graphical frame. The **Image** data type is capable of handling the following image file formats:

- Bitmaps (.BMP)
- Graphics Interchange Format (.GIF)
- Joint Photographic Experts Group (.JPEG or .JPG)
- Portable Network Graphics (.PNG)
- Tag Image File Format (.TIFF)

The image type that you use does not really matter for this course. There are positives and negatives for each type. Bitmaps (.BMP) are the most simplistic of the image types, but they tend to be fairly low-quality when compared to other types. Portable Network Graphic (.PNG) files have the best quality of image, but tend to be very large files. JPEGs and GIF files have middle-quality images and file sizes. Our game programs will use either JPEG, GIF or PNG formats.

The first step to using an image in the program is to create your **Image** variable:

```
Dim myImage As Image
```

Now that you have created a variable of type **Image** called **myImage** you need to load the image file into this variable. There are two main ways to do this: loading the image by filename, or attaching the image as a resource to your project and then using the resource name.

Using Image.FromFile()

The **Image.FromFile()** function allows you to load a specific filename into the **Image** variable like this:

```
myImage = Image.FromFile("c:\myimage.jpg")
```

The parameter to the method is the path (including filename) to your file. The example above assumes that the "myimage.jpg" file is in the root (or main) directory of the C drive. You would have to type the correct location for any image file that you want to load.

Using Resource Files

It may not be practical to hard-code in a specific file name and path if you don't know where your program will be installed or where the images will actually be located on the computer. Instead, a more convenient technique is to add your image files to your Visual Basic project as **resource** files. Resource files are automatically copied to the build directory along with the executable files when the program is compiled and built. These files can be accessed by name through the **My.Resources** object, as the following "Walking Man" example will demonstrate.

Walking Man

Let's create a project and learn how to add images as resources into our project. You will use this project again in the next lesson.

To begin, open the Visual Basic 2010 Express IDE and create a new project called "Walking Man". Change the **(Name)** property to "WalkingForm" and the **Text** property to "WalkingMan". Save this project in the activity starter directory: "**\KidCoder\Game Programming\Activity Starters\Walking Man**". (The Walking Man directory already exists in that spot because we have provided some image files for you).

To add your images, click on the "Project" menu item and then click on "Walking Man Properties".

Next click on the word "Resources" on the left side of this screen. This should bring up the screen shown to the right.

The drop-down combo box near the top left lets you pick different types of resources. If you don't see "Images", click on that box and change from "Strings" or other resource type to "Images".

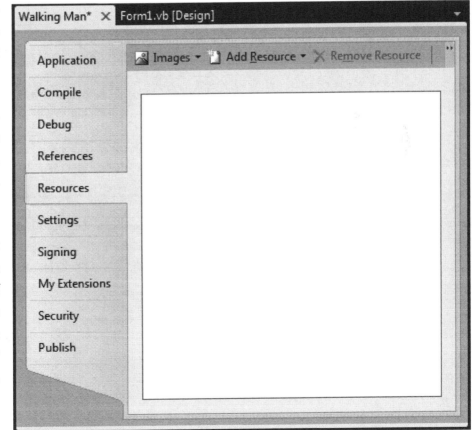

Now you can click on the little arrow to the right of the "Add Resource" button at the top of the screen, which will bring up the following menu:

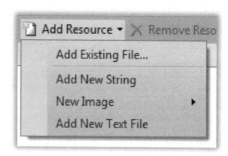

We want to add some existing files, so click on the "Add Existing File" item to bring up the "Add existing file" dialog.

Here you can choose the file or files that you want to add as a Resource to your project. For this project you want to add the Walking Man images that you will find in your "**\KidCoder\Game Programming\Activity Starters\Walking Man\Images**" directory. You should find eight images called "walking1.gif", "walking2.gif", etc. Once you have selected your files, you can click on "Open" and the files will be added to the project as resources!

You should see your images listed under the Resources folder in your Solution Explorer pane.

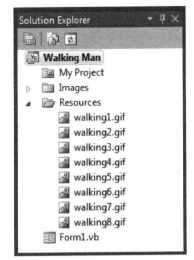

Once these files have become resources in the project, you can just ask for them by name in your code using the **My.Resources** prefix:

```
Dim myImage As Image = My.Resources.walking1
```

The above code will load the "walking1.gif" image into your **myImage** variable. Now you don't have to remember in what directory or hard drive your images are stored!

Now that we have a frame loaded into our **Image** variable, we need one last piece of information before we can display it to the screen: We need to know *where* on our form to draw our image. The location of an image is determined by its upper-left point. So where do you want to put your image? It depends on where your game needs the image to appear. For now we will just start our image at point (100,100). Use a **Point** data type to hold our upper-left coordinate:

```
Dim startingPoint As Point = New Point(100,100)
```

Next, we need to display our image on the screen. All image drawing is done within the form's **Paint** method using the **Graphics** object. Create your **Paint** subroutine and add the following code:

```
Private Sub WalkingForm_Paint(ByVal sender As Object, _
                    ByVal e As System.Windows.Forms.PaintEventArgs) _
                    Handles Me.Paint
    ' assuming you already initialized myImage & startingPoint somewhere
    ' else in the program, draw the image using Graphics.DrawImage()
    Dim myGraphics As Graphics = e.Graphics
    myGraphics.DrawImage(myImage, startingPoint)
End Sub
```

It's very simple to display an image. Use the function **DrawImage**() on the Graphics object which takes two parameters: the name of the **Image** variable, and a **Point** where the image will be drawn.

Notice that you don't want to create a new **Image** object each time the **Paint** method is called. It could take a long time to reload the file from disk each time you paint it. It's better to load the images or resources once (perhaps in the Form **Load** function) and then just use the **Image** variables afterwards.

That's all there is to loading and displaying an image from a file! In the next lesson, we will discuss how to animate a series of images in a program.

Lesson Three: Animation with Timers

In this lesson, we will show you how to animate the images that you have created and loaded into your program.

The key to simple game animation in Visual Basic is the Timer event. If you make a timer event fire at a fast enough rate, and you change your image every time the timer fires, you have created an animation!

Walking Man Continued

You are going to continue working with the "Walking Man" program created in the last lesson. We want Walking Man to cycle through eight hand-drawn images of a walking man. When these images are cycled at about 13 frames a second (a timer interval of 75), the figure will appear to walk in place on the screen!

To begin, open the Visual Basic 2010 Express IDE and load the project that you created in the last lesson. You should be able to find this project in your "**\KidCoder\Game Programming\Activity Starters\Walking Man**" directory.

Next, add an array of **Images** called `walkingManImage` which will hold your eight frames. Also add an **Integer** variable `currentMan` which will hold the current index of the image which should be displayed on the screen. You can create the variables right underneath your main form so they are visible everywhere in the program.

```
Public Class WalkingForm
        Dim walkingManImage(7) As Image
        Dim currentMan As Integer = 0
```

Next, add a Timer for your project by choosing the Timer control from the toolbox and dragging it onto your form. Once you have created your timer, change the **(Name)** to **WalkingTimer** and change the **Interval** to 75 milliseconds.

Create a function to handle the Form **Load** event (by double-clicking on the form in the design screen or using the combo boxes at the top of the code screen). In the **Load** event, you should prepare the timer and the image array:

- Load each of the eight images into the **walkingManImage** array.
- Start the timer with the **WalkingTimer**.**Start**() command.

When done, your **Load**() function should look like this:

```
Private Sub WalkingForm_Load(ByVal sender As Object, _
                         ByVal e As System.EventArgs) Handles Me.Load

    walkingManImage(0) = My.Resources.walking1
    walkingManImage(1) = My.Resources.walking2
    walkingManImage(2) = My.Resources.walking3
    walkingManImage(3) = My.Resources.walking4
    walkingManImage(4) = My.Resources.walking5
    walkingManImage(5) = My.Resources.walking6
    walkingManImage(6) = My.Resources.walking7
    walkingManImage(7) = My.Resources.walking8


    WalkingTimer.Start()

End Sub
```

Next, create the Timer **Tick** subroutine. Within this subroutine you will need to:

- Add one to the value of the **currentMan** variable. This is the index into the **walkingManImage** array. The value should be a number between 0 and 7 since you have an 8-element array. If the **currentMan** value is greater than 7, you want to set it back to 0.
- Call the **Invalidate**() function, which will cause the form's **Paint** function to be called after each timer event fires.

Your final **Tick** subroutine should look like this:

```
Private Sub WalkingTimer_Tick(ByVal sender As System.Object, _
                        ByVal e As System.EventArgs) Handles WalkingTimer.Tick
    ' Increment current frame index by one
    currentMan = currentMan + 1


    'If the current man index is greater than our last image,
    'change back to the 0th image
    If (currentMan > 7) Then
        currentMan = 0
    End If
End Sub
```

Finally, create the **Paint** event handler function. In this function you will actually draw the image for the current frame! Draw the image on the screen at location 100,100 with the Graphics **DrawImage()**. Here is your completed function:

```
Private Sub WalkingForm_Paint(ByVal sender As Object, _
            ByVal e As System.Windows.Forms.PaintEventArgs) Handles Me.Paint

    Dim myGraphics As Graphics = e.Graphics
    Dim startingPoint As Point = New Point(100, 100)
    myGraphics.DrawImage(walkingManImage(currentMan), startingPoint)

End Sub
```

Now when you build and run your program you should see the animated walking man cycle through all 8 images!

Advanced Animation Tips

You may have noticed a couple of visual annoyances when watching your Walking Man program in action!

First, the image may seem to flicker a little bit at random times. This may happen when the image is being updated by the program at the same time it is displayed on the computer screen. There is a setting on the form you can change that will help eliminate this problem. From the form design window, right-click on the form and select "Properties". Then scroll down to the **DoubleBuffered** property and change the value from **False** to **True**. This tells the program to draw the entire image first before displaying it on the computer screen. You should always set the **DoubleBuffered** property to **True** for any of your programs that will be using animated graphics, or even non-animated images that are moved across the screen!

Second, you can see that the background of the walking man images is white, and the default background of the form is a light gray. This won't look so good in a game if your animated pictures all have a background that does not match the overall background of the form! There are a couple of ways you can fix this.

The simplest solution is to change the background color of your form to match the background color of the images (in this case white). To do this, find the **BackColor** property of the form and change the color to White. Now when you build and run the program the entire screen should be white and you can't tell where the edges of the walking man images begin.

But what if you have more than one animation on the screen, and the background color of each is different? You only have one form background color and can't change it to match everything at once. The solution is to identify the background color of the **Image** as "transparent" when you call **DrawImage**(). That way the color of the main form background will show through everywhere your image's background color would normally used to be!

 Not all image types support transparency! The most common transparent images are created as either GIF or PNG files. These types will allow you to display transparent parts of an image or drawing. Other types like JPG or BMP will NOT allow you to set transparency!

The parameters to **DrawImage**() to set a transparent color are unfortunately a bit more complicated than the earlier version.

```
Public Sub DrawImage (image As Image, destRect As Rectangle, _
                      srcX As Integer, srcY As Integer, _
                      srcWidth As Integer, srcHeight As Integer, _
                      srcUnit As GraphicsUnit, imageAttr As ImageAttributes)
```

Here is the meaning of each parameter:

image	This is just your **Image** variable
destRect	This rectangle should contain the upper-left coordinate where you want the image to appear on the screen and the width and height of the image. You can use the **image.Width** and **image.Height** for width and height.

srcX, srcY	The srcX and srcY parameters should be set to 0, 0 to show you want to start drawing from your source image at the image's upper-left corner.
srcWidth, srcHeight	The srcWidth and srcHeight parameters should be set to **image.Width** and **image.Height** to show that you want to draw all of the source image.
srcUnit	The srcUnit parameter should always be **GraphicsUnit.Pixel**
imageAttr	See below

The **ImageAttributes** are the key to selecting a transparent background color! You can create the attributes parameter as follows (this example uses White, but you can pick any color in your image as transparent):

```
Dim imageAttr As ImageAttributes = New ImageAttributes
imageAttr.SetColorKey(Color.White, Color.White)
```

You will also have to add an **Imports** line for the "System.Drawing.Imaging" library at the top of your form if it's not already there:

```
Imports System.Drawing.Imaging
```

Now let's put this all together in a new call to **DrawImage** that will use white as the transparent color!

```
Dim imageAttr As ImageAttributes = New ImageAttributes
imageAttr.SetColorKey(Color.White, Color.White)

Dim myImage As Image = walkingManImage(currentMan)
Dim destRect = New Rectangle(100, 100, myImage.Width, myImage.Height)
myGraphics.DrawImage(myImage, destRect, 0,0, myImage.Width, myImage.Height, _
                GraphicsUnit.Pixel, imageAttr)
```

That's quite a lot of code, but when you build and run your program you'll notice it's worth it! The Walking Man image's white background is gone and you can see the form's background showing through the image.

 **Chapter Review**

- Computer animation is the process of quickly showing different images, giving the illusion of motion.

- Flipbook animation is a good way to test an animation idea before doing the full artwork.

- Images may be stored in different file formats such as: BMP, GIF, JPEG, PNG, or TIFF.

- Visual Basic uses the **Image** data type to load images from files and assign to variables.

- To load an image into an **Image** variable, you can call the **Image.FromFile()** function.

- Instead of using **Image.FromFile** you can also add the images to your Visual Basic project as a resource, then assign to your Image variable from **My.Resources**.<imageName>.

- The Timer is a very important tool when performing computer animation.

- The Timer event is used to change the current image and **Invalidate()** the screen so **Paint** will be called fast enough to give the illusion of movement.

- The **Paint** method is responsible for drawing the image on the screen using **DrawImage**.

- The simplest **DrawImage** function needs an **Image** variable and a starting point, which represents the upper-left point for your image.

- Set the Form's **DoubleBuffered** property to **True** to help eliminate annoying flicker.

- Use an advanced form of **DrawImage** to set a transparent background color within your **Image**.

Your Turn! Your Own Animation

In this activity, you will create your own animation with your own images. Here is what you will need to do:

- Create or find a series of images (preferably GIF files) which show some sort of action, for example:
  - A flower blooming
  - A flag waving
  - A face which goes from frowning to smiling
  - A stick man being drawn
- Make sure all of your images are the same size.
- Add your images as resources into the Walking Man program.
- In the form's **Load** event, change the "walking1" through "walking8" images names to your new image resources.

Now run your program. How do your new images look? If you are creating your own images, don't be discouraged if it takes you a few tries to make them flow smoothly together. Animation is a fine art form, and we're more focused on learning how to make it work in a computer program!

You might find your images online, or you can create your own using the Windows Paint program. If you can't get or create a new set of images, you may use the images from the activity solution, which show a series of faces changing from happy to a sad face.

Chapter Seven: Sprites

In this chapter we will discuss one of the most important building blocks of any game: sprites. We will also begin building a new game to put our sprites to good use!

Lesson One: Sprite Concepts

What is a *sprite*? In game programming, a sprite is a graphical object on the screen that we can move and manage with our code. Sprites can be simple, fixed objects or complicated, animated, movable objects that can collide with one another. A single game can have any number of sprites. Sprites can represent your good guys, bad guys, ships, missiles, walls, and so on.

 In game programming, a sprite is not a refreshing drink! A sprite can be any graphical object on the screen. A spaceship, ping-pong ball, and a rock are all possible examples of game Sprites.

Although your sprites may each look very different, you will find that writing the code behind them requires the same basic set of tasks each time. Any sprite may need to move, speed up, slow down, bounce off a wall, or display an animated image.

Instead of writing lots of the same code to handle each sprite individually, most game programs use a sprite library as part of their game logic. For this course we provide a sprite library for you! The sprite library defines a new **Sprite** data type you can declare as a variable. The **Sprite** contains properties to represent the object's size, position, speed, image, and other parameters. The **Sprite** also contains functions that will make the sprite move, collide, rotate, and other useful features. By using a sprite library you will be able to write programs more quickly and easily instead of re-inventing the wheel within each program!

In the next two chapters we will describe several important sprite concepts and show how those concepts are supported by our **Sprite** library. Along the way you will be developing a fully functional "Bubble Blaster" game with the techniques you have learned!

The Sprite Library

Our **Sprite** library is contained in a code file called "SpriteLibrary.vb". This file will be present in each of your Activity Starter projects. During the next few chapters we will show you how this library works. Once we are done you will have a fully-featured **Sprite** library that can be used in any game program!

To use the **Sprite** library, first you need to add the file "SpriteLibrary.vb" to your project. This is done by clicking on the Project menu and then choosing "Add Existing Item".

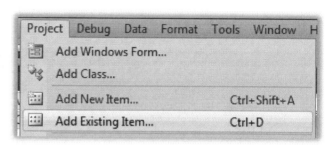

Then you just need to find the directory with the "SpriteLibrary.vb" file and add that file to the project.

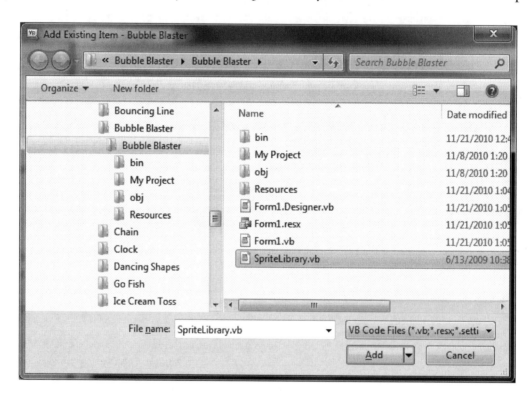

This step is already done for you in all of the Activity Starter projects, but when you write your own games you will have to do it yourself!

Once you have the **Sprite** library file added to the project, you can then create as many variables as you like where the data type is **Sprite**:

```
Dim mySprite As Sprite = New Sprite()
```

Notice that you have to use the **New** keyword to create a new copy of the **Sprite** to store in the variable!

Sprite Positioning and Size

Sprites are visual objects you see on the screen. Sprites therefore must have some properties describing their position and size. The position is represented by the same X and Y coordinates we have worked with in previous chapters. Since we are representing the position of a sprite with a single pair of coordinates, we need to know which part of the sprite those coordinates represent. Sprites are usually positioned using the coordinates of the upper-left corner of the sprite. If the sprite is not a rectangle, you can mentally draw a rectangle around the outer edges of the sprite shape. This rectangle is called a bounding rectangle. The sprite is then located using the upper-left corner of the bounding rectangle.

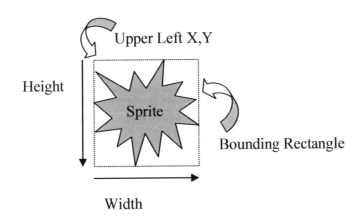

The **Sprite** library contains a function called **GetBoundingRectangle**(), which will return a **Rectangle** with the **Sprite's** location coordinates, width, and height.

```
Public Function GetBoundingRectangle() As Rectangle
```

Using the **GetBoundingRectangle**() function is pretty simple. For example:

```
Dim boundingRectangle As Rectangle
boundingRectangle = mySprite.GetBoundingRectangle()
```

This will provide you with a rectangle that represents the sprite's boundaries on the screen. Since this information is often useful in your game logic, you will find that the **GetBoundingRectangle**() function comes in real handy!

So far you have learned about two properties of a sprite: *position* and *size*. These properties are part of the **Sprite** data type as follows:

```
Public UpperLeft As Point
Public Size As Point
```

Both properties are **Points**, which means they have an X and Y component. The **UpperLeft** Point represents the screen coordinates of the upper left corner. The **Size** Point represents the width (X) and height (Y) of the sprite.

When you want to get or set the **Sprite** size or position just read or set the **UpperLeft** and **Size** properties with new values. In this example we set the position to (50, 100), the width to 20, and the height to 30.

```
    ' set the sprite position to (50,100)
    mySprite.UpperLeft.X = 50
    mySprite.UpperLeft.Y = 100


    ' set the sprite size to width = 20, height = 30
    mySprite.Size.X = 20
    mySprite.Size.Y = 30
```

Sometimes you may find it more convenient to get or set the sprite position in terms of the sprite's center instead of the upper-left corner. Our **Sprite** library has functions that will do that too!

```
    Public Sub SetCenter(ByVal center As Point)
    Public Function GetCenter() As Point
```

You can call those methods on your sprite objects as follows:

```
    ' get the sprite's current center location
    Dim myCenter = mySprite.GetCenter()

    ' set the sprite's new location using the center point at (200,150)
    myCenter.X = 200
    myCenter.Y = 150
    mySprite.SetCenter(myCenter)
```

Setting Sprite Images

Sprites are almost always represented as an image on the screen. This means that we must be able to set and display the Sprite's image in a game program.

The Sprite Library contains two different methods for setting the Sprite's image: **SetImage()** and **SetImageResource()**. The method that you choose to use depends on how you will be adding the images to your game program.

If you simply want to load the image from a file on your hard disk, you can use the **SetImage()** method. This method looks like this:

```
SetImage(filename As String)
```

To use this method, you can simply pass in the name of an image on your computer, like this:

```
mySprite.SetImage("c:\myimage.jpg")
```

The example above assumes that the "myimage.jpg" file is in the root (or main) directory of the C drive. You would have to type the correct location for any image file that you want to load. This method is similar to the **Image.FromFile()** method mentioned in the previous chapter.

If you have chosen to add your images to your project as resources, you can use the **SetImageResource()** method to set your Sprite's image. This method looks like this:

```
SetImageResource(resourceName As System.Drawing.Image)
```

To use this method, you will pass in the name of your image resource:

```
mySprite.SetImageResource(My.Resources.myImage)
```

This will load a resource called "myImage" into your Sprite. In general, using resources is better than using filenames for your game images. Resource files will actually become part of the game program when it is compiled and built in the IDE. This means that you do not have to worry about copying images in order to play the game on different computers.

Painting Sprite Images

In order to paint a sprite's image on the screen, you can use the **Sprite.PaintImage()** function. This function takes two parameters: a **Graphics** object, which represents the paintable area of the game screen and a **Boolean** value which represents the transparency of the image. If the value is **True**, the image is drawn with transparency. If the value is **False**, the image is not drawn with any transparency.

```
PaintImage(myGraphics As System.Drawing.Graphics, transparent As Boolean)
```

To use this method, you could use a line of code like the following one:

```
mySprite.PaintImage(myGraphics, True)
```

This would paint the Sprite's image, with transparency, to a Graphic object called **myGraphics**. Remember that in order to use transparency, an image must be of type GIF or PNG!

Lesson Two: Introducing Bubble Blaster

Over the next few chapters you will be writing a complete game -- Bubble Blaster! This game will show off many important sprite concepts and is fun to play! Here is an example screenshot of what the finished game will look like:

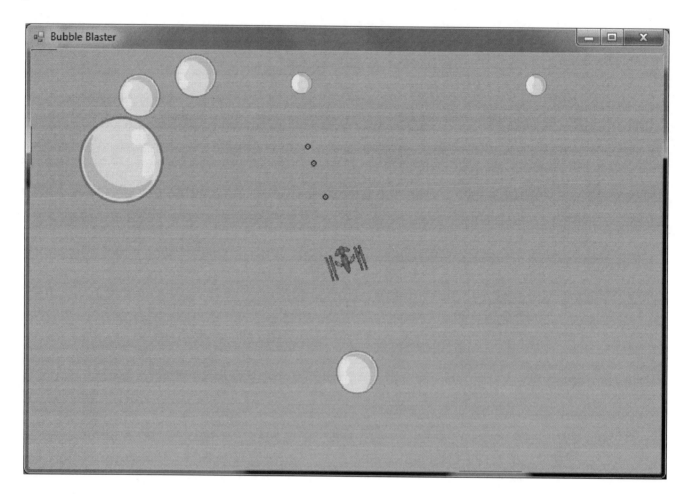

Game Play

Let's first take a look at what the game of Bubble Blaster is all about.

The Bubble Blaster game is similar to a popular arcade game called "Asteroids". "Asteroids" was originally released by Atari in 1979. The game was both simple and addictive. When the game begins, you see a spaceship, shaped like a simple triangle, in the middle of the screen. Floating around this spaceship is a series of large asteroids. These asteroids will float and spin in random directions around the screen.

In our Bubble Blaster game the ship is attempting to pop bubbles which are floating around the ship.

The objective of Bubble Blaster is simple: you need to shoot the bubbles around you without letting any of them hit your ship. If any bubble hits your ship, your game is over. To shoot at the bubbles, you can hit the fire button, which will send out a single shot from the front of the spaceship each time the button is pressed. You can also spin your ship around in a full circle and move forward in the direction you are facing.

When you hit the large bubbles with your shots, the bubble will break into two smaller bubbles. When any of these medium-sized bubbles are hit, they will break into two even smaller bubbles. When you shoot these smaller bubbles, they will just disappear. The game is over when all the bubbles are cleared from the screen or until your ship is hit by a bubble.

Bubble Blaster Activity Starter

You will have to program a number of important features within the Bubble Blaster game as new skills are introduced in the following lessons and chapters. However, you don't have to start from scratch! We provide a Bubble Blaster Activity Starter project that takes care of some of the boring parts for you. As we complete lessons you will fill in specific functions in order to make things happen on the screen.

The starter project for this activity can be found in your "**KidCoder\Game Programming\Activity Starters\Bubble Blaster**" directory. The name of the solution is "**Bubble Blaster.sln**". Go ahead and open up the Visual Basic 2010 Express software and load this solution.

The activity starter project includes the following elements:

- The main screen form named **BlasterForm**
- All of the images necessary for this game
- All of the variables in the game state are already created for you
- The **Sprite** library is included in the project and **Imported** at the top of the form
- A timer has been added to the form
- Several functions are pre-defined for you – no need to change any of these methods!
- Some functions are empty -- these will be your responsibility!

The following constant variables are declared at the top and will set things like the ship speed and number of bubbles that will appear. We will learn to use these over the next couple of chapters as we add more features to the game!

```
' maximum ship speed, acceleration rate
Const MAX_SHIP_SPEED As Double = 15.0
Const SHIP_ACCELERATION As Double = 1.5

' shot speed and lifespan
Const SHOT_SPEED As Double = 20.0
Const SHOT_TIME_TO_LIVE As Integer = 15

' speed of big, medium, and small bubbles
Const BIG_BUBBLE_SPEED As Double = 2.0
Const MED_BUBBLE_SPEED As Double = 3.0
Const SML_BUBBLE_SPEED As Double = 4.0

' number of big bubbles to start
Const NUM_BIG_BUBBLES As Integer = 3

' maximum number of ship shots that can be on the screen at once
Const MAX_SHIP_SHOTS As Integer = 5
```

The following functions are completely finished already and you won't have to change them. We'll give a short description here and you can review the code in the activity starter if curious about those parts of the game. Don't worry if some features are strange right now; you will understand them all very soon!

Function Name	Description
BlasterForm_Load()	When the program is first run the form **Load** method will call **StartGame**()
StartGame()	Performs the steps to initialize all of the game data and start the timer
StopGame()	Performs the steps to stop the game and display a message to the user
BlasterTimer_Tick()	The timer tick will move sprites, check for collisions, and process keys
BlasterForm_Paint()	Draws the bubbles, ship, and shots on the screen
PaintShip()	Draws the ship image, correctly rotated in the direction the ship is facing
ExplodeBubble()	Called when a ship's shot hits an bubble
CreateSmallerBubble()	Called from **ExplodeBubble**() when we want to create a new smaller bubble

The rest of the functions are empty and you will complete them over the next couple of chapters as we finish each lesson. Here is a brief description of what each function will do:

`InitializeBubbles()`	Creates and initializes the sprites in the bubbles array
`PaintBubbles()`	Draws the bubble images on the screen
`MoveBubbles()`	Moves bubbles according to their current direction and speed
`InitializeShip()`	Create the ship sprite and initialize the ship's angle, speed, and position
`BlasterForm_KeyDown()`	Keeps track of which keys are pressed down by the user
`BlasterForm_KeyUp()`	Keeps track of which keys are released by the user
`ProcessKeys()`	Rotates the ship, accelerates, or shoots according to the keys held down
`MoveShip()`	Moves the ship according to its current direction and speed
`InitializeShots()`	Creates and initializes the sprites in the shots array
`Shoot()`	Find an available shot in the shots array and initialize it to the current position
`MoveShots()`	Moves shots according to their current speed and direction
`PaintShots()`	Draws active shots on the screen
`CheckShipCollisions()`	Determines if the ship has hit any bubble
`CheckShotCollisions()`	Determines if any active shots have hit any bubble
`CheckIfWinner()`	Determines if the player has destroyed all of the bubbles on the screen

 If you build and run the activity starter as-is without making any code changes, you won't see anything on the screen and nothing will happen when you press any keys. Never fear, you will get things going quickly!

Your Turn! Starting Bubble Blaster

The first thing you will do to improve the Bubble Blaster game is create some bubbles to show on the screen! To do this you will complete the functions **InitializeBubbles()** and **PaintBubbles()**. Open the "**Bubble Blaster.sln**" in your Visual Basic 2010 Express software so we can get to work!

Note that this project uses a "random number generator" to choose a random location on the screen for our bubbles. Visual Basic contains a special object which easily creates random numbers called **System.Random**. We have already created a variable of this type (called **RandomNumGen**) at the top of the Bubble Blaster code. In order to get a new random number, we will call the **Next()** method on this variable and tell the method the highest possible number that it can choose. For example, take a look at the following code:

```
RandomNumGen.Next(Me.ClientSize.Width)
```

This will choose a random number between 0 and the width of the screen. This enables us to choose a random location from left to right for our bubble. Since this is a new object for you, we will give you the code line to use when necessary!

InitializeBubbles

Find the **InitializeBubbles()** function in your Bubble Blaster project. All of the code you will write for Bubble Blaster will be in the "Form1.vb" source file.

```
Private Sub InitializeBubbles()
End Sub
```

InitializeBubbles() is called from the **StartGame()** method which is already completed for you. To initialize the bubbles, you will first need to know where they are stored! The activity starter declares this array of **Sprites** at the top of the form to hold the bubbles:

```
Dim bubbleArray(NUM_BIG_BUBBLES - 1) As Sprite
```

This **bubbleArray** will grow as you play the game because new bubbles are created. So, to start out, we want to **ReDim** the array back to the starting size. Add this line at the top of your **InitializeBubbles()** function:

```
ReDim bubbleArray(NUM_BIG_BUBBLES - 1)
```

Now, you need to add code to create and initialize the properties of a new **Sprite** for each of the elements in the **bubbleArray**. Create a **For** loop with an index that goes from 0 to NUM_BIG_BUBBLES – 1.

Within the loop, for each element in the **bubbleArray** you should:
- Create a new bubble **Sprite** and store it in the array
- Use the **Sprite.SetImageResource()** function to set the image to: "My.Resources.bubble_large"
- Set the bubble's **UpperLeft.X** position to a random value. The activity starter already has a random number generator at the top of the form: **RandomNumGen**. You can use it to pick random value between 0 and the screen's width like this:

```
bubbleArray(i).UpperLeft.X = RandomNumGen.Next(Me.ClientSize.Width)
```

- Set the bubble's **UpperLeft.Y** position to another random value between 0 and the screen's height:

```
RandomNumGen.Next(Me.ClientSize.Height)
```

At this point when you run your program you still won't see anything on the screen. That will change when you implement **PaintBubbles()**!

PaintBubbles

The **PaintBubbles()** function is called from the main **Paint()** method that is already done for you in the activity starter. As you might guess, this function will need to draw all of the bubbles on the screen!

```
Private Sub PaintBubbles(ByRef myGraphics As Graphics)
End Sub
```

To paint the bubbles, you will simply need to call the **PaintImage()** function on each **Sprite** in the **bubbleArray**.

Create a **For** loop that will loop over each element of the **bubbleArray**. Note that the size of the array will change over time as bubbles are shot and explode into smaller bubbles. So you don't want to loop to a constant like NUM_BIG_BUBBLES as you did during **InitializeBubbles()**. Instead loop using the current size of the array like this:

```
For i = 0 To bubbleArray.Length - 1
```

Within the loop for each bubble you should:

- Call the bubble's **PaintImage()** function, passing in the **Graphics** object and **True** to have the image drawn with transparency.

 Now when you build and run your program you should see 3 big bubbles created on the screen in some random position! We'll learn how to make them move in the next lesson.

Lesson Three: Sprite Movement

In this lesson we will learn about sprite direction, speed, and acceleration.

Sprite Direction

Our sprites will be able to move in any direction on the screen. This means that they can be moving to the right, left, up, down or at some other angle. We will store the sprite's direction as an angle, measured in degrees between 0 and 360. These angles are similar to using a compass to determine your direction.

To understand which direction an angle represents, consider the circle diagram below. By convention 0 degrees is always pointing to the right, 90 degrees points straight up towards the top of the circle, 180 degrees points directly to the left, and 270 degrees will always point straight down. There are of course many angles between these four points. Angles between 0 and 90 represent some direction pointing up and to the right. Similarly, angles between 90 and 180 point up and to the left, and so on.

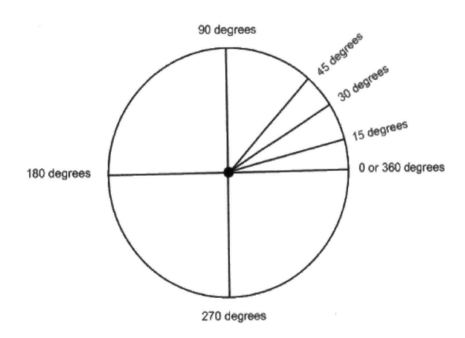

The angles of a circle move from 0 to 360 in a counter-clockwise direction. When you get all the way up to 360 degrees you have reached your starting point directly to the right, and start over at 0 again.

The **Sprite** library we provided for you will internally use trigonometry functions on the angle to calculate how far to move in the X and Y directions. For those calculations we will convert the angles in degrees to angles in radians (another measuring system for angles). You don't have to worry about the math behind the calculations, but if you are looking at the **Sprite** library code just be aware that conversion is taking place. You will always use degrees between 0 and 360 to set the **Sprite** direction and rotation.

Speed and Velocity

Moving sprites on a screen is a lot like giving someone directions to your house. If someone asks you for directions, you can't just tell them that you live five miles away. (Not and expect them to show up, anyway!) You need to give them both a distance and a direction, like "five miles northwest".

The same thing is true when you need to move a sprite on the screen. Each time the timer ticks you want to move the sprite some number of pixels as determined by the sprite's current speed. However, you can't just tell the sprite to move five pixels. The sprite would not have any idea what direction to move! Instead you want to move the sprite a certain number of pixels (speed) in a certain direction (angle). This combination of speed and direction is called *velocity*. You can also represent velocity as movement in both X and Y directions (e.g. 3 pixels up and 4 pixels right).

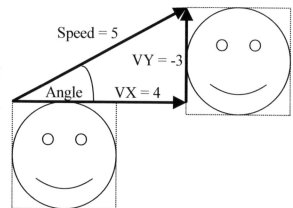

In the diagram to the right we see that the sprite speed is 5 at a certain angle. When moving the sprite (by adjusting the upper-left corner position!) we can equivalently move the sprite 4 pixels in the X direction and -3 pixels in the Y direction. Remember that in computer terms the "up" direction is negative and the "down" direction is positive.

Given a speed and any angle between 0 and 360 degrees we can calculate the X and Y velocity (VX and VY) that will tell us how many pixels to move the sprite in each direction. The math to perform these calculations requires a bit of trigonometry so we won't detail it here. Don't worry; the **Sprite** library will do all this work for you! If you are curious you can review the code inside the **Sprite** movement functions.

Acceleration

The speed of an object is the distance the object can travel over a certain amount of time. For example, the speed of a car may be measured in the number of miles or kilometers it travels in an hour. Acceleration is a measure of how fast you are speeding up or slowing down. If you step on the gas pedal in a car, the car will increase its speed, or accelerate. If you step on the brake pedal, the car will slow down, or decelerate. The rate that the car speeds up or slows down is its acceleration or deceleration. So, for instance, if your car is travelling at 20 miles per hour and you accelerate 5 miles per hour, the car will end up travelling at 25 miles per hour (the original speed plus the acceleration).

Graphical objects on the screen can also accelerate and decelerate. Let's say you have a simple program in which a dog walks across the screen. When the program starts the dog is moving at a speed of 5 pixels a second. Now let's say the dog is being chased by a dog catcher. The program allows the user to hit the plus key (+) to accelerate the dog by 2 pixels each time the key is pressed. If the user hits the key 3 times then the dog's speed is accelerated to 5 + 2 + 2 + 2 = 11 pixels a second! Voila! The dog can escape the evil dog catcher.

You usually want to accelerate an object in one of two ways. First, in many cases the acceleration is working along the same angle as the sprite is moving. The car example falls into this case, where acceleration (or breaking, which is just negative acceleration) always happens in whatever direction the car is heading. You can simply specify a single acceleration value that should impact the sprite's overall speed.

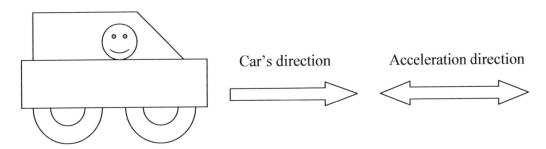

In other cases your sprite may be subject to acceleration that is not in the same direction as it is traveling. For instance, consider a beach ball that is thrown into the air. The ball is certainly going to be affected by gravity which is a steady acceleration in the downwards direction. The ball also may be affected by some wind which is acceleration in the horizontal direction. In this case you don't necessarily know the impact on the overall speed of the ball, or the ball's direction. However you can say for certain how strong the gravity is in one direction and how string the wind is in another direction. You can apply the two acceleration components to the ball's X and Y velocity values and effectively change the direction and speed of the ball.

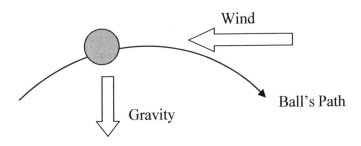

The **Sprite** library allows you to accelerate an object using both of these techniques, so pick whichever one is most useful for the type of sprite in your game!

Sprite Movement Properties and Functions

Now that you understand direction, velocity, and acceleration, let's look at the movement properties and functions in our **Sprite** library.

There are three properties you can set related to movement:

```
Public Angle As Double
Public Velocity As PointF
Public MaxSpeed As Double
```

The **Angle** is a number between 0 and 360 degrees and represents the direction the sprite is currently traveling. The **Velocity** is a point representing the X and Y velocity components (VX and VY in our diagrams). The **MaxSpeed** is a number representing the fastest overall speed that the sprite will be allowed to move. If you do not set this value, the user may be able to accelerate a sprite until its motion is too fast to control!

There are four methods that allow you change the sprite's speed and direction:

```
Public Sub SetVelocity(speed As Double)
Public Sub ChangeAngle(delta As Double)
Public Sub Accelerate(acceleration As Double)
Public Sub Accelerate(AX As Double, AY As Double)
```

The **SetVelocity()** method allows you to specify the overall speed for your sprite, and the function will calculate the **Velocity** X and Y components automatically based on your current **Angle**.

The **ChangeAngle()** method will adjust (add to) your current **Angle** by the specified amount which can be either positive or negative. A positive angle change will rotate the sprite to the left. A negative angle change will rotate the sprite to the right. The angle is automatically wrapped to stay between 0 to 360 degrees.

The first **Accelerate** () method with one parameter fits the case where acceleration is to be applied (either positive or negative) in the current direction of travel. The overall acceleration is broken down into X and Y components based on the **Angle** and applied to the **Velocity** X and Y values.

The second **Accelerate()** method with two parameters fits the case where we know certain X and Y acceleration components already and just need them applied to the **Velocity** X and Y values.

Finally, here is a very important method that actually moves your sprite across the screen!

```
Public Sub MoveAndWrap(screenSize As Point)
```

This method will update your sprite's current position (**UpperLeft** property) based on its current **Velocity**. What happens if your sprite moves all the way off the form's screen? That's where the "wrap" part of the function comes into play! Your parameter to this function is a **Point** representing the current size of your screen (usually **Me.ClientSize**). If the sprite's position falls outside that width and height boundary it will be automatically wrapped around to the other side of the screen!

Now let's take a look at some examples using these properties and functions!

```
mySprite.Angle = 90        ' set the sprite's direction to point straight up
mySprite.Velocity = New Point(0,0) ' set sprite's VX and VY to zero
mySprite.MaxSpeed = 10     ' set the sprite's max overall speed to 10
```

When the **Accelerate()** function is called, a new X and Y speed will be calculated for the sprite based on the sprite's acceleration value and the current speed. To use this function, you just call it in your program:

```
mySprite.SetVelocity(5)      ' set the sprite's overall speed to 5
mySprite.ChangeAngle(10)     ' add 10 degrees to the current sprite Angle
mySprite.ChangeAngle(-10)    ' subtract 10 degrees from current sprite Angle
mySprite.Accelerate(3)       ' accelerate sprite by 3 along current Angle
mySprite.Accelerate(-.5, .5) ' accelerate with specific X and Y values
```

Note that the size of your acceleration values will determine how fast or slow the sprite will change speeds. If you want to speed up slowly, these numbers will be small. If you want to speed up quickly, these numbers will be larger.

Finally, to move a sprite along the current direction using the current velocity:

```
mySprite.MoveAndWrap(Me.ClientSize)
```

Now that you understand how to make a sprite move, let's return to Bubble Blaster and put those bubbles into motion!

117

Your Turn! Ships and Bubbles

The next thing you will do to improve the Bubble Blaster game is add the spaceship and get those bubbles moving around the screen! To do this you will add a few things to **InitializeBubbles()** and complete the **MoveBubbles()** function. You will also set up the player's space ship in the **InitializeShip()** function.

InitializeBubbles()

In the last activity you implemented **InitializeBubbles()** to give all of the initial bubbles some location and size. Now we need to enhance that method to also assign a direction, speed, and max speed! Go back to **InitializeBubbles()** and, within your **For** loop, set the following two **Sprite** properties for each bubble:

- Set the **Angle** using "**RandomNumGen.Next**(0,360)" function to get a random angle between 0 and 360 degrees

- Set the **MaxSpeed** property to the constant BIG_BUBBLE_SPEED because all of the initial bubbles are of the "big" size and will move at a constant speed.

- Finally, you also need to call the **SetVelocity()** method on each sprite to assign a speed of BIG_BUBBLE_SPEED in the current direction.

MoveBubbles()

MoveBubbles() is called from the timer tick method that was provided for you in the activity starter. Each time the timer ticks we want to move the bubbles a little bit! Find the **MoveBubbles()** function in your activity starter:

```
Private Sub MoveBubbles()
End Sub
```

Remember that all of our bubble sprites are stored in the **bubbleArray**. In your implementation of **MoveBubbles()** you should loop over the **bubbleArray** with a **For** loop. The **For** loop should use the current length of the array to calculate the upper bound and not a fixed constant, as the number of bubbles in the array will change over time.

Within the **For** loop on each sprite you simply need to:
- Call the sprite's **MoveAndWrap()** method

Don't forget to pass in the **Me.ClientSize** property to **MoveAndWrap()** so the **Sprite** library knows your current screen dimensions!

At this point when you run your program you should see the bubbles flying around the screen in random directions. When they reach the edge of the screen they should automatically wrap to the other side!

InitializeShip()

The **InitializeShip**() method is called from the **StartGame**() function and is responsible for setting up the sprite for the players space ship.

```
Private Sub InitializeShip()
End Sub
```

The activity starter has already declared a variable to hold the ship sprite at the top of the form:

```
Dim myShip As Sprite
```

You will fill in the **InitializeShip**() function to create a new **Sprite** for **myShip** and set the initial properties. Specifically, you will need to:

- Set the image to "My.Resources.BBShip" using **SetImageResource**()
- Set the **MaxSpeed** to MAX_SHIP_SPEED
- Calculate the center point of the screen:
  - Create a new variable called **centerPoint** as a **Point**.
  - Set **centerPoint**.X equal to **Me.ClientSize.Width** / 2
  - Set **centerPoint**.Y equal to **Me.ClientSize.Height** / 2
  - Now your **centerPoint** variable represents the center of your game screen!
- Call the sprite's **SetCenter**() method with **centerPoint** in order to position the ship exactly in the middle of the screen.

When you build and run your program, you should now see the space ship displayed in the middle of the screen, pointed to the right. The bubbles are still flying around, but you can't move your ship or shoot at anything...yet!

In the next chapter you will learn how to change user key presses into ship movement, how to fire shots, and how to detect collisions between sprites!

Chapter Review

- A sprite is a graphical object on the screen that you can move and manage with code.

- Sprites can be simple fixed objects or complicated animated and interactive objects.

- A single game can have many different sprites.

- The **Sprite** library is an object we provide that contains many functions and properties that are common to all sprites.

- Each **Sprite** has properties that determine the location and size.

- You can assign an image resource to a **Sprite** using **Sprite.SetImageResource**().

- You can draw a **Sprite** on the screen using **Sprite.PaintImage**().

- Each Sprite has an **Angle** property that determines which direction it is moving on the screen.

- Angles are measured in degrees from 0 to 360.

- An angle of 0 degrees means pointing directly to the right.

- The speed of an object is the distance the object travels in a certain time (e.g. 50 miles per hour).

- The velocity of an object combines its speed with a direction.

- The acceleration of an object is the rate of increase in its speed. The deceleration of an object is the rate of decrease in its speed. Deceleration can be represented by a negative acceleration value.

- Be sure to use the **New** keyword to create a new **Sprite** and assign it to your variable.

- You can create an array of sprites just like you create an array of any other data type.

All of the Your Turn activities for this chapter have already been completed during the chapter lessons!

Chapter Eight: Game Logic

In this chapter we will apply some of the skills you have already learned to finish the Bubble Blaster game. Most of the building blocks are in place; now you will implement the game logic to tie it all together. Along the way we will develop some new concepts such as collision detection and limited sprite life-spans.

Lesson One: Controlling the Ship

In this lesson we will use keyboard input to control the space ship in the Bubble Blaster game. Our space ship needs to be able to turn and accelerate to move around the screen. The key to steering the ship and shooting at bubbles is the ability to rotate or spin the ship left and right.

Our game will use the following keys to control the ship:

- The left arrow key will rotate the ship in a counter-clockwise direction.
- The right arrow key will rotate the ship in a clockwise direction.
- The up arrow key will accelerate the ship in whatever direction it is pointing.
- The space bar will launch a shot in the ship's current direction

Handling Many Keys at the Same Time

Many arcade games allow players to press several keys at once for a combination of effects. Bubble Blaster is no exception! Our players will want to move, steer, and shoot all at the same time. In order for this to work we need to track the "up" or "down" state of each key we're interested in.

Your activity starter project has these pre-defined variables to track the key states:

```
    ' these boolean variables track which key(s) are currently down at any time
Dim keyLeftPressed As Boolean
Dim keyRightPressed As Boolean
Dim keyUpPressed As Boolean
Dim keySpacePressed As Boolean
```

There are five important functions that will work together to implement key press logic:

BlasterForm_KeyDown()	Sets a key pressed variable to **True** when the key goes down
BlasterForm_KeyUp()	Sets a key pressed variable to **False** when the key goes up
ProcessKeys()	For each key currently held down, perform the action for that key (ship rotate, accelerate, or fire shots)
MoveShip()	Move the ship in the current direction at the current speed
BlasterTimer_Tick()	Calls **ProcessKeys()** method each timer tick to detect which keys are down and execute the actions for each key that is down. Calls the **MoveShip()** method each timer tick so the ship will move.

You will make the first four functions work in an upcoming activity! The **BlasterTimer_Tick()** method is provided for you and described in the next section.

BlasterTimer_Tick

The heart of any arcade game is the timer "Tick" function that gets called many times a second. For this game we have set the timer interval to 100 milliseconds, which means the **BlasterTimer_Tick()** method is called 10 times a second. This is fast enough to give the illusion of smooth movement across the screen and respond quickly to user key-presses.

The **BlasterTimer_Tick()** method is already implemented for you in this project. However it's important to understand what's going on inside so you can write your own for future games!

```
Private Sub BlasterTimer_Tick(ByVal sender As System.Object, _
                ByVal e As System.EventArgs) Handles BlasterTimer.Tick


' (timer tick game logic implemented here)
End Sub
```

Our tick method performs these general tasks:

- Process all of the keys that are currently held down - makes the ship move, shoot, etc.
- Move all of the sprites on the screen - ship, bubbles, and shots
- Check for collisions between the ship and bubbles or between the shots and bubbles
- Determine if the game is over and, if so, display a message to the user
- Invalidate the screen so it will be repainted, showing all of the sprites in their new position.

In the next activity, you will implement the logic for the other four methods related to key presses and ship movement!

Your Turn! Ship Movement

All activities in this chapter will build on the Bubble Blaster game that you began in the last chapter. Go ahead and run Visual Basic 2010 Express and open the Bubble Blaster project.

In this activity you will give the player the ability to move the ship around the screen! As described above, there are four different functions involved, plus a timer tick method that ties them all together. The tick function has been completed for you, so you just need to complete the remaining four functions.

BlasterForm_KeyDown()

Remember that we have defined some Boolean variables to track when certain keys are held down:

```
' these boolean variables track which key(s) are currently down at any time
Dim keyLeftPressed As Boolean
Dim keyRightPressed As Boolean
Dim keyUpPressed As Boolean
Dim keySpacePressed As Boolean
```

Find the empty **BlasterForm_KeyDown** function in your project:

```
Private Sub BlasterForm_KeyDown(ByVal sender As Object, _
        ByVal e As System.Windows.Forms.KeyEventArgs) Handles Me.KeyDown


End Sub
```

Now write code within the **BlasterForm_KeyDown**() method as follows:
- If the user is pressing the left arrow key, set the **keyLeftPressed** flag to **True**.
- If the user is pressing the right arrow key, set the **keyRightPressed** flag to **True**.
- If the user is pressing the up arrow key, set the **keyUpPressed** flag to **True**.
- If the user is pressing the space bar, set the **keySpacePressed** flag to **True**.
- (Hint: Use the **Select** statement instead of the **If** statement. Review the keyboard input lesson from Chapter 4 if necessary!)

BlasterForm_KeyUp()

Next you need to implement the **BlasterForm_KeyUp()** method.

```
Private Sub BlasterForm_KeyUp(ByVal sender As Object, _
            ByVal e As System.Windows.Forms.KeyEventArgs) Handles Me.KeyUp


End Sub
```

Go ahead and write the code in function to do just the opposite of the **BlasterForm_KeyDown** logic:

- If the user has let up the left arrow key, set the **keyLeftPressed** flag to **False**
- If the user has let up the right arrow key, set the **keyRightPressed** flag to **False**
- If the user has let up the up arrow key, set the **keyUpPressed** flag to **False**
- If the user has let up the space bar key, set the **keySpacePressed** flag to **False**

ProcessKeys()

The third function you will implement is **ProcessKeys()**. In this function you should check the state of each of the key pressed flags. If any of these flags are **True**, you will need to perform the correct action for that key.

Remember that the left and right arrow keys will rotate the ship, and that the ship's direction can be adjusted by calling the Sprite's **ChangeAngle()** method with a positive or negative angle value. You can control how fast or slow the ship rotates by using a larger or smaller angle adjustment. We suggest 10 degrees as a reasonable number but you can experiment with other values to see the effects on rotation speed!

You also want to check for the "up" arrow. If that arrow is pressed then we want to make the ship move faster by calling the Sprite's **Accelerate()** function. You can control how fast you want your ship to accelerate by adjusting the **SHIP_ACCELERATION** constant that is defined at the top of the source code. A larger value will make the ship gain speed very quickly as the up arrow is pressed, while a smaller value will make the ship accelerate more slowly. We suggest 1.5 as a reasonable number but you can adjust that value to change the way the ship flies!

Finally, we need to check to see if the space bar is being held down. If so we want to fire a shot! We haven't discussed exactly how that will work yet, but there is a **Shoot()** method that has already been created for you. If the space bar is down, just call the **Shoot()** function and we'll worry about the details later.

Here is a summary of what you have to do inside **ProcessKeys**():

- If the **keyLeftPressed** flag is **True**, call the ship Sprite's **ChangeAngle**() function with a parameter of +10
- If the **keyRightPressed** flag is **True**, call the ship Sprite's **ChangeAngle**() function with a parameter of -10
- If the **keyUpPressed** flag is **True**, call the ship Sprite's **Accelerate**() function with the value of the **SHIP_ACCELERATION** constant
- If the **keySpacePressed** flag is **True**, call the **Shoot**() method.

MoveShip()

The last function you have to finish is **MoveShip()**.

```
Private Sub MoveShip()

End Sub
```

Fortunately, this is also the easiest! We have already initialized the ship's position, speed, and direction. We have also already implemented the key handling logic to change those things according to the player's wishes. All that's left is to move the ship along its current direction using its current speed. To do this, from within **MoveShip**() just call the **myShip.MoveAndWrap**() function. Don't forget to pass in **Me.ClientSize** (the current size of the screen) so the ship will wrap from one edge of the screen to the opposite side.

 After these four functions are finished you can build and run your program. You should now be able to control your ship with the arrow keys! Notice that the space bar doesn't do anything yet because we haven't written the Shoot() method or initialized the Sprites that make up the actual shots.

Lesson Two: Sprite Life-spans

Sometimes you may have sprites on your screen that don't last very long. The Bubble Blaster ship's shots are a great example. They are only visible for a couple of seconds before expiring. It may not be smart to repeatedly create and destroy new **Sprite** objects each time a shot appears and disappears, however. Let's look at a new feature of our **Sprite**: the life-span or "Time-To-Live" (TTL).

The **Sprite's** time-to-live is controlled by a counter. Each time the **Sprite** moves the counter is reduced by one. When the counter gets to zero the sprite is "dead". Once a **Sprite** becomes "dead" it is no longer visible on the screen and cannot collide with any other **Sprite**.

Sprite Library Time-To-Live

The **Sprite** library supports the Time-To-Live feature with these two properties:

```
Public IsAlive As Boolean = True
Public TimeToLive As Integer = -1
```

The **IsAlive** property is normally **True**, which means the **Sprite** is visible on the screen and can collide with other **Sprites**. If the **IsAlive** property is **False**, the sprite is not visible on the screen and it cannot collide with or interact with any other sprite.

The **TimeToLive** property is the life-span counter. If you want the **Sprite** to be always alive then just leave the counter at the default -1. This means the **Sprite** will not have a limited lifespan. However if you want the sprite to only appear for a little while, set the **TimeToLive** counter to some positive value. Each time the sprite moves the counter will be reduced by one. When the counter hits zero then the **IsAlive** property is automatically set to **False** and the sprite will disappear from the screen.

How can you tell what value to use in the initial **TimeToLive** counter? If the counter will be reduced by one each time the **Sprite** moves, and the **Sprite** moves once each time the timer tick event happens, then you can calculate how fast your counter will decrease based on the timer interval. In the Bubble Blaster game, the timer fires 10 times a second. So if you initialize the **TimeToLive** value to 20 then the sprite would last 2 seconds (20 divided by 10) on the screen before disappearing.

Ship Shots

Since the ship shots have a position, size, direction and need to be moved around the screen, we will use **Sprite** objects for each one. Since we could have a bunch of shots on the screen at the same time, we will actually use an array of **Sprites**. The player can only have as many shots on the screen at one time as we allow in our array! This prevents a user from shooting constantly and filling up the entire screen with shots. Like all of our other arrays, we will create the maximum number of shots as a constant (**MAX_SHIP_SHOTS**), so we can easily change the number of shots later.

```
' All ship shots are contained in this array of Sprites
Dim shipShots(MAX_SHIP_SHOTS - 1) As Sprite
```

When the spaceship shoots, the shot will travel in a straight line in the direction that it was launched until it hits a bubble or until the time-to-live counter runs out. If a shot hits the edge of the screen before it runs out of time it will wrap around the screen just like the bubbles and the ship.

There are five important functions that will work together to implement the shots:

InitializeShots()	Creates all of the Sprites in the **shipShots** array
Shoot()	Finds an empty (dead) shot in the **shipShots** array and fires it from the ship
PaintShots()	Draws any live shots as a small rectangle on the screen
MoveShots()	Calls **MoveAndWrap()** on each live shot to move them on the screen
BlasterTimer_Tick()	Calls **MoveShots**() method periodically so the shots move.

You will implement the first four functions in the next activity!   **BlasterTimer_Tick**(), as we already described, has been done for you.

Your Turn! Ready, Aim, Fire!

In this activity, you will add the ability to create ship shots and move them across the screen! As described above, there are four different functions that perform specific tasks, plus a timer tick method that ties them all together. You will need to complete the following four functions, plus add some code to the **PaintBubbles**() method we worked on in an earlier activity.

InitializeShots()

The **InitailizeShots**() function will be called when the game starts, from the **StartGame**( ) function.. Here is where you will initialize all of the elements of the **shipShots** array with **Sprites** ready to be used!

```
Private Sub InitializeShots()

End Sub
```

Find the **InitializeShots**() function in your project, then finish it with the following logic:

- Create a **For** loop to go over each of the elements in the **shipShots** array
- For each element
    - Create a new **Sprite** and assign it to the element
    - Set the **Sprite.IsAlive** property to **False** (all shots are initially inactive!)
    - Set the image to "My.Resources.shot" using **SetImageResource**()
    - Set the Sprite's **MaxSpeed** to SHOT_SPEED as they will travel at that constant speed

Shoot()

The **Shoot**() function is called from **ProcessKeys**() each time we detect that the space bar is held down. **Shoot**() will attempt to find a dead (or available) sprite in the **shipShots** array, If all shots are currently active then the user cannot fire any more shots, and the **Shoot**() function doesn't do anything. If an available shot is found you will fire a new shot as follows:

- Create a **For** loop to iterate over each of the elements in the **shipShots** array
- For each element
    - If the sprite's **IsAlive** property is **False**

- Set the sprite's **IsAlive** property to **True**
- Set the sprite's **TimeToLive** property to SHOT_TIME_TO_LIVE
- Set the sprite's **Angle** property to the ship's angle (**myShip.Angle**)
- Set the sprite's Velocity to SHOT_SPEED using the **SetVelocity()** method
- Set the sprite's **UpperLeft** position to the center of the ship by using the **GetCenter()** function on the ship sprite.
- Exit the **For** loop immediately using the **Return** statement. This will ensure we only fire one shot at a time and avoid activating all of the available shots at once!

PaintShots()

The **PaintShots()** function is called by the main **BlasterForm_Paint()** function, which was already completed for you. Find the **PaintShots()** function in your program:

```
Private Sub PaintShots(ByRef myGraphics As Graphics)
End Sub
```

All we need to do in **PaintShots()** is draw the shot images on the screen. Go ahead and complete this function as follows:

- Create a **For** loop so you can check each of the shots in the **shipShots** array.
- For each shot:
  - If the shot is alive
    - Call the shot's **PaintImage()** function, passing in the **myGraphics** object and **True** to have the image drawn with transparency.

MoveShots()

The **MoveShots()** function is almost as easy as the **MoveShip()** function you completed earlier. The only difference is you have a bunch of shots to move instead of one ship!

```
Private Sub MoveShots()
End Sub
```

Finish this method now by writing the following code:

- Create a **For** loop that will loop through the **shipShots** array.
- For each shot in the **shipShots** array
  - Call the sprite's **MoveAndWrap()** function, passing in the form's **Me.ClientSize**

PaintBubbles

We need to make one quick addition to the **PaintBubbles**() function you finished earlier. Now that it's possible to shoot the bubbles and make them disappear, we will need to make sure each bubble is "alive" before we paint it on the screen. Inside your **For** loop in this method, add an **If** statement around the **PaintImage**() line of code to see if the bubble's **IsAlive** value is **True**. Only call the **PaintImage**() function if the bubble is currently alive!

 Now, when you build and run the program you should be able to shoot a number of shots across the screen! The shots should appear to be fired from the nose of your ship in the direction the ship is facing. After a couple of seconds they will disappear. You should have a limited number of shots that can be active at any one time.

Notice that no matter how hard you try, the shots don't seem to have any effect on the bubbles. That's because we haven't learned about collision detection yet! The next lesson will describe how sprites collide with (or hit) one another.

Lesson Three: Collision Detection

A typical game will involve many sprites moving around the screen at the same time. So what happens when two sprites run into each other? Maybe a race car has crashed into a chicken, or a shot has hit a target, or a ball has been hit with a racquet. When any of these things happen, we need to perform some action in our game: a ball that has been hit with a racquet needs to bounce back across the screen, a target that has been shot requires a change in score, and a chicken that has been hit by a race car is, well, one really mad chicken!

In order to know if any of our sprites have hit each other we will use a process called "collision detection". *Collision detection* is simply a check of all sprites on the screen to see if anyone has crashed into anyone else.

The simplest method of collision detection is to look at the bounding rectangles of all our sprites. If any of the bounding rectangles intersect (meaning, any point on or within one rectangle touches any part of the other rectangle) then we decided that those two sprites have collided.

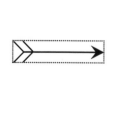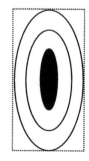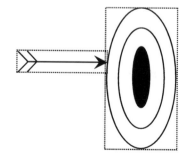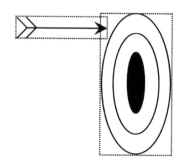

The drawing above shows two sprites: an arrow and a target. The dotted lines represent the bounding rectangles of each sprite. In the first picture the rectangles clearly do not intersect, so there is no collision. In the second picture the rectangles do intersect, so there has been a collision! In the third picture notice that the rectangles intersect yet the actual graphical arrow does not yet reach the circular target. Nonetheless we still declare this a collision! At game speeds with objects moving around such a collision is "close enough" to be counted, and the player hopefully will not notice the tiny mistakes in the collision detection logic. Although not perfect, the bounding rectangle collision detection is very simple to implement!

Sprite Library Collision Detection

Since almost every game may want to detect collisions we have added support for collision detection in the **Sprite** library. You can call the **IsCollided**() method on a **Sprite** and pass in another **Sprite** as the parameter. The function will return **True** if the sprites are collided or **False** if they are not. Here are the function details:

```
Function IsCollided(ByRef otherSprite As Sprite) As Boolean
```

If we had already defined an **arrowSprite** and a **targetSprite**, we could just call this function on one sprite (the arrow) and pass in another sprite (the target) as a parameter like this:

```
Dim isCollided as Boolean = arrowSprite.IsCollided(targetSprite)
```

If the two sprites have hit each other (their bounding rectangles have overlapped), the return value will be **True**; otherwise it will be **False**. Notice is doesn't matter on which sprite you call the function and which sprite you pass in as the parameter. This statement will return exactly the same results:

```
Dim isCollided as Boolean = targetSprite.IsCollided(arrowSprite)
```

Your Turn! Damage Control

Now it's time for you to write the code to detect collisions between the ship and the bubbles and between the shots and the bubbles. When the ship collides it's obviously bad news for the player! When the shots collide with bubbles we will break them down into smaller bubbles or remove them completely from the screen. You will complete two functions: **CheckShipCollisions**() and **CheckShotCollisions**().

CheckShipCollisions()

The **CheckShipCollisions**() function is called by the timer tick method after all of the sprites have moved. This function should check for collisions between the ship and all of the bubbles on the screen.

```
Private Sub CheckShipCollisions()
End Sub
```

Find the **CheckShipCollisions**() function in your project and add code as follows:

- Start with a **For** loop that examines each element in the **bubbleArray**.
  - Remember that the current size of the **bubbleArray** changes over time, so your **For** loop should loop from 0 to **bubbleArray**.**Length** - 1
- Within the **For** loop, check each bubble for a collision against the **myShip** sprite using the **IsCollided**() method.
- If there is a collision, we want to "destroy" the ship. You can do this by setting the ship sprite's **IsAlive** property to **False**.

- After your **For** loop is complete, look at the ship's **IsAlive** property to see if the ship was destroyed. If **IsAlive** is equal to **False**
  - Call the **StopGame**() method. This method has already been written for you and will perform the necessary steps to stop the game and display some message to the user.
  - Pass in some descriptive string to **StopGame**() telling the user that the ship has been destroyed. For example:

```
StopGame("Your ship has been destroyed!")
```

 Now when you build and run the game your ship should collide with any bubble that gets in its way, and your descriptive game-over message will be displayed to the user. The shots still won't break up those pesky bubbles, which obviously isn't fair! So let's write that logic next.

CheckShotCollisions()

The **CheckShotCollisions**() function is very similar to **CheckShipCollisions**(). However instead of just one ship we have an entire array of shots! Some, all, or none of the shots in the array might be active at any given point. Your function code needs to loop through both the shots array and the bubbles array, calling the **IsCollided**() function to see if any shots have collided with any bubbles.

```
Private Sub CheckShotCollisions()
End Sub
```

In order to check all the elements of one array against all the elements of another array, you'll need two **For** loops– one within the other. Here is some starter code to get you going:

```
For i = 0 To MAX_SHIP_SHOTS - 1      ' for each ship shot

    For j = 0 To bubbleArray.Length - 1 ' examine each bubble

        ' Check for collisions here!

    Next
Next
```

Notice we are using the **i** loop variable for the **shipShots** array, so you would access each shot sprite as **shipShots(i)**. The **j** loop variable is for the bubbles array, so you would access each bubble as **bubbleArray(j)**.

Inside the inner loop, you will need to check to see if **shipShots(i)** has collided with **bubbleArray(j)**.

If they have collided, you need to:

- Call the **ExplodeBubble()** function and pass in the bubble that was hit (**bubbleArray(j)**).
    - The **ExplodeBubble()** function has already been completed for you, and just takes care of the boring logic that breaks down a larger bubble down into two smaller bubbles, or removes a small bubble from the screen entirely.
- Show that the shot is now "dead" by setting the shot sprite's **IsAlive** property to **False**.
    - Once that shot is declared dead, the program may re-use that spot in the **shipShots** array for another new shot the next time the player hits the space bar.

That's all there is to collision detection in the Bubble Blaster game!

 Now when you build and run the program you should be able to blast those bubbles right out of the sky! Your game is almost done, congratulations!

The next lesson will finish the logic that detects when the player has won the game.

Lesson Four: Winning the Game

At this point your player can do just about everything they need to within the Bubble Blaster game -- fly, shoot, collide, and so forth. The last important missing element is ending the game! For our simple game we will declare the player a winner when all of the bubbles have been shot off the screen. The timer tick function already calls a **CheckIfWinner()** function after moving and colliding all of the sprites. You will need to finish this function to check all of the bubbles to see if any are left alive. If not, the player is a winner!

Your Turn! Victory at Last

In this activity you will complete the Bubble Blaster game logic by writing the **CheckIfWinner()** function.

```
Private Sub CheckIfWinner()
End Sub
```

The player has "won" the game if all of the bubbles are destroyed. So your function code should simply loop over the bubbles array checking to see if any bubbles are still alive. If at least one bubble is alive then the game is not over. If all bubbles are dead then the game is over and you can declare the winner.

Within the **CheckIfWinner()** function, you should:

- Create a **Boolean** variable called **isAnyoneAlive** and set it to **False**.
    - This variable will track whether or not at least one bubble is still alive.
- Create a **For** loop over the bubbles array (remember to use the current array length)
    - Check each bubble sprite's **IsAlive** value
    - If the bubble is alive, set **isAnyoneAlive** to **True**.
- After the loop has finished, check the value of the **isAnyoneAlive** variable.
    - If the value is **False**, then there are no more bubbles on the screen, so:
        - Call the **StopGame()** function with the message: "You Win!"

That's it! At this point, you have written a real, working Bubble Blaster game. Go ahead and try out your skill!

Chapter Review

- Use a timer to generate tick events many times per second. You will write most of your game logic within the tick function, or within functions called by the tick function.

- To support more than one key press at the same time, you should use a tracking flag for each of the keys you want to process.

- Use the KeyUp and KeyDown events to set or clear the tracking flag for each key.

- The **Sprite.TimeToLive** property is a counter which tracks how long the sprite is "alive" on the screen.

- The **Sprite.IsAlive** property determines if the sprite is "alive" and visible on the screen.

- You can detect if two sprites have collided by seeing if their bounding rectangles intersect.

- The **Sprite.IsCollided()** function is used to tell whether or not two sprites have collided.

- Make sure to detect when the player has won or lost the game, and display a message letting them know what has happened!

All of the Your Turn activities for this chapter have already been completed during the chapter lessons!

Chapter Nine: Sound

So far we have learned about the graphics that make computer games look great. But there are other special effects important to computer games besides graphics. Sound and music, for instance, can turn a good game into a fantastic experience! In this chapter we will learn how to play sound effects and background music.

Lesson One: Simple Sounds

There are several ways to play sounds in Visual Basic. In this lesson, we will learn about the simplest form of sound a computer can make: beeps. The early computers used for the first games did not have sound cards. In fact, sound cards did not become a part of a normal computer until the 1990s. Earlier computers only had a PC speaker which could make beeping sounds. This speaker was intended to give simple feedback when a computer had an error. But computer game programmers hijacked the PC speaker when they began writing games in the 1970s and 1980s. These programmers figured out that if you make small changes to the duration and frequency (pitch) of the beep, you can make simple musical notes. These notes were then used to make music and special sound effects in a game.

 **The sound card was not widely used until the late 1980s. Even then, it was used mostly for creating and playing simple music and speech. It wasn't until the 1990s that sound cards were used to enhance computer games with more realistic sounds.**

Today's computers usually have built-in sound cards that are capable of playing realistic sounds in different formats. However, some game programmers still choose to use the beeps from a PC speaker. Why? Beeps are fast and easy to add to a computer game and don't need a sound card to be present in the computer.

So how do we make a computer beep with Visual Basic? There are two ways.

Sound Card Beeps

To make your sound card play a beep sound, you can just call the **Beep**() function like this:

```
Beep()
```

That's it! Every time you call that function, your computer will give a sort of beeping sound. This is an easy way to add a simple beep to your program. However, it does not actually make the beep sound through your PC speaker. Instead, it makes the beep through your sound card! Since there are no parameters to the function you do not have any control over the pitch or duration of this sound -- you're stuck with whatever noise the sound card makes.

PC Speaker Beeps

How do we make music with the beeps from the PC speaker? We use a different function called **Console.Beep()**. This will actually make a sound through your PC speaker. This function also allows us to change the pitch (frequency) and duration of the sound as follows:

```
Console.Beep(soundFrequency, soundDuration)
```

The first parameter **soundFrequency** is an integer value which controls the pitch of the sound that you want to play. This value can be anything between 37 and 32767. Lower numbers give a low-pitched sound. Higher numbers give a higher-pitched sound.

The second parameter **soundDuration** is an integer value which sets how long you want your beep to last. This value is counted in milliseconds, so a value of 1000 is 1000 milliseconds or one second, and a value of 500 is 500 milliseconds or half of a second.

 **Your Turn! Mary had a Little Lamb**

In this activity you will create a program that has a single form and a single button. When the user clicks the button, you will use the **Console.Beep()** function to play the song: "Mary Had a Little Lamb".

The starter project for this activity can be found in your "**\KidCoder\Game Programming\Activity Starters\Marys Lambs**" directory. The name of the solution for this chapter is "**Marys Lambs.sln**". Go ahead and open up Visual Basic 2010 Express and load this solution.

The starter project contains the following elements:

- A form called **MaryForm** that has the caption "Mary Had a Little Lamb"
- A button named **PlayButton** that has the text "Play Song".

- Constant values for the following note frequencies:

```
Const G_BELOW_C As Integer = 784
Const A As Integer = 880
Const B As Integer = 988
Const D As Integer = 1175
```

- Constant values for the note durations that you will need:

```
Const WHOLE_NOTE As Integer = 1600
Const HALF_NOTE As Integer = WHOLE_NOTE / 2
Const QUARTER_NOTE = HALF_NOTE / 2
```

To complete this activity, add calls to the **Console.Beep**() function in the **PlayButton.Click**() event. The following notes should be played in order (bold notes are "half notes", all others are "quarter notes"):

B, A, G_BELOW_C, A, B, B, **B**,   ("Mar-y had a lit-tle lamb,")

A, A, **A**,   ("lit-tle lamb,")

B, D, **D**,   ("lit-tle lamb,")

B, A, G_BELOW_C, A, B, B, **B**,   ("Mar-y had a lit-tle lamb,")

B, A, A, B, A, **G_BELOW_C**   ("Whose fleece was white as snow.")

When you click the "Play Song" button, you should hear a simple version of this song!

 In rare cases, a computer may not have the right hardware to make any noise when you use Console.Beep()! If you call Console.Beep() and don't hear anything, you can skip this activity and continue on to the next lesson. The sound functions in the next lesson will work on all computers with sound cards.

Lesson Two: Loading and Playing Sound Files

In the last lesson we learned about the simple sounds you can make using the **Beep** functions. However, in some games, you may want to play more complicated sounds through your sound card. These sounds or music are stored in sound files on your computer. For this course, we will be using a type of audio file called a Waveform Audio File or ".WAV" file (pronounced "wave"). These files can hold *uncompressed* audio. Other sound formats exist such as .MP3 and .WMA, but those formats hold *compressed* audio. Compressed audio files are more difficult to use because they must be decompressed before being played through a sound card. Most .WAV files are already in a decompressed format that can be directly played, so we will only be working with uncompressed WAV audio files.

SoundPlayer

To play a WAV file in your program, we will be using the **SoundPlayer** object. **SoundPlayer** is part of a library called "System.Media". The System.Media library should be imported into any program that wants to use the **SoundPlayer**. This statement should be placed above the **"Public Class** FormName" line in your form's code:

```
Imports System.Media
```

The first step to using the **SoundPlayer** object is to declare and initialize a variable of this type in your program:

```
Dim mySoundPlayer As SoundPlayer = New SoundPlayer
```

Now we have created a new variable called **mySoundPlayer** and assigned to it a new **SoundPlayer**. Next, we want the **mySoundPlayer** object to load the audio file that contains the sound we want to play. There are two ways you can load a sound from disk into your **SoundPlayer**!

Loading Files by Location

If you know the location of your WAV file on your hard drive you can set the **SoundLocation** property of **SoundPlayer** to point to that location as follows:

```
mySoundPlayer.SoundLocation = ("c:\mySound.wav")
```

This statement will load the file "mySound.wav" in the "C:\" directory to our new **SoundPlayer**.

Once we have an audio file loaded into our **SoundPlayer**, we can simply play the file like this:

```
mySoundPlayer.Play()
```

If you have a sound that you want to play over and over in your game (like background music), you can replace the **Play** function with the **PlayLooping** function:

```
mySoundPlayer.PlayLooping()
```

To stop the playback of any sound, you can call the Stop function:

```
mySoundPlayer.Stop()
```

Loading Files as Resources

What if you don't know the location of your sound file when writing the code? A better way to load an audio file is to create an embedded resource, just like we did for the image files in an earlier chapter. This means that the audio file actually becomes part of your project and you don't have to worry about locating the file on the hard drive; you can just reference it by resource name.

To add a sound file as a resource, click on "Project" on the top menu and then choose "Project Name Properties". (Note: "Project Name" will be the actual name of your project.)

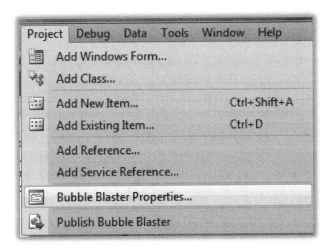

Then click on the Resources tab on the left side of the properties window. You should now see two buttons at the top with little arrows next to them. The left button controls the type of resource (String, Audio, Images, etc). Make sure that is set to "Audio" for sound files. Then click on the "Add Resource" button and choose "Add Existing File".

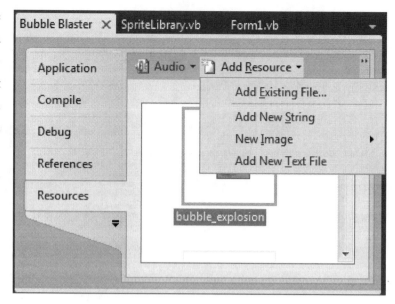

Now use the next dialog screen to find WAV file on the hard drive and click "Open" to add it as a resource.

When you are done, you should see a new item called "Resources" in your Solution Explorer. Your WAV file should be listed under this item.

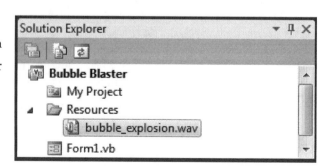

Now you can use your new audio resource! Instead of setting the **SoundPlayer.SoundLocation** property to load the file, you set the **SoundPlayer.Stream** property equal to **My.Resources**.<sound name>. For example, if you loaded "bubble_explosion.wav" as a resource, you can set the **Stream** as follows:

```
mySoundPlayer.Stream = My.Resources.bubble_explosion
```

Notice that you do not need to use the file extension (in our case the .wav) in the resource name. The program knows what kind of a file it is, so no need to type it in here!

Once you assign a resource to the **Stream** property, you can use the same **SoundPlayer** methods that we described above: **Play()**, **PlayLooping()** and **Stop()**.

Using System Sounds

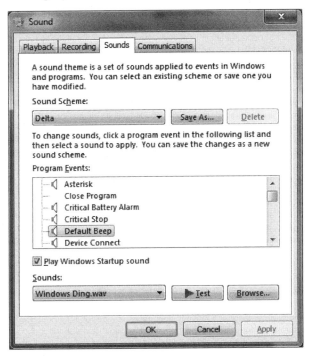

Sometimes you may want to play an existing Windows system sound instead of something you provide in a file. System sounds are the sounds that Windows plays whenever some event happens, such as an error pop-up. These sounds are defined in your Windows Control Panel under "Sounds and Audio Device Properties". An example Control Panel screen for some versions of Windows is shown to the left.

You will notice that some of the sounds have a speaker icon next to them and some of them do not. The ones without a speaker icon do not have any sound linked with them, so these system events will not make any noise.

Visual Basic allows you to use the most common system sounds:

Asterisk or Beep	The most common system sound is the **Asterisk** sound. Windows will play the **Asterisk** sound whenever an important message box appears or an error happens. The **Beep** sound is sometimes used for the same thing.
Exclamation	The **Exclamation** sound is typically heard when a serious error occurs in a Windows program. You may have heard this sound when your Visual Basic program has an error.
Help or Question	The **Help** or **Question** sound is typically heard when a Help window is shown on the screen.

When you want to get your user's attention by using one of these system sounds you will declare and initialize a variable of type **SystemSound** (instead of **SoundPlayer**). You initialize the **SystemSound** variable from one of the following values:

- **SystemSounds.Asterisk**
- **SystemSounds.Beep**
- **SystemSounds.Exclamation**
- **SystemSounds.Help**
- **SystemSounds.Question**

When you initialize your variable, instead of creating a new **SystemSound**, you can just assign it one of those predefined values. For example:

```
Dim mySystemSound As SystemSound = SystemSounds.Asterisk
```

Once you create the **SystemSound** variable you can call the **Play** method like this:

```
mySystemSound.Play()
```

That's it! Playing system sounds in a program is very simple.

Lesson Three: Adding Sound to Bubble Blaster

In this lesson we will begin creating sound effects in your Bubble Blaster game! Go ahead and run Visual Basic 2010 Express and open the Bubble Blaster project that you have been working on in the last couple of chapters.

We will add a sound effect for the ship shooting, the bubbles exploding, the ship accelerating and for when the ship is destroyed. These four sound WAV files can be found in your "**\KidCoder\Game Programming\Activity Starters\Bubble Blaster\Sounds**" directory.

- bubbles_accelerate.wav
- bubbles_shot.wav
- bubbles_shipdestroyed.wav
- bubble_explosion.wav

The first step is to add your sound files to the project as resources. This keeps us from having to remember where the sound files are on our hard drive.

To add a sound file as a resource, click on "Project" on the top menu and then choose "Bubble Blaster Properties". Then click on the Resources tab on the left side of the properties window. Make sure the resource type is "Images", click on the arrow next to the "Add Resources" button, and choose "Add Existing Resource". Then find the provided WAV files in the "Bubble Blaster\Sounds" directory and add them as resources. When you are done, you should see the WAV files should be listed under the Resources area in your Solution.

Once the sounds are added to the project, we can use them in our program. The starter activity for the Bubble Blaster game contains a **SoundPlayer** variable for each sound declared at the top of the form:

```
Dim shotSound As SoundPlayer = New SoundPlayer
Dim explodeSound As SoundPlayer = New SoundPlayer
Dim accelerateSound As SoundPlayer = New SoundPlayer
Dim gameOverSound As SoundPlayer = New SoundPlayer
```

You should also find a function called **InitializeSounds()**. This function will be used to assign the sound resources to the **SoundPlayer** variables.

```
Private Sub InitializeSounds()
End Sub
```

In this function, we initialize each **SoundPlayer** variable by setting the **Stream** property equal to a **My.Resources** name. Once we initialize the sounds they are ready to play when we need them!

Go ahead and find the **InitializeSounds**() function in your project, and add the following lines:

```
shotSound.Stream = My.Resources.bubbles_shot
explodeSound.Stream = My.Resources.bubble_explosion
accelerateSound.Stream = My.Resources.bubbles_accelerate
gameOverSound.Stream = My.Resources.bubbles_shipdestroyed
```

That's all we need to do to initialize the sounds for our game. **InitializeSounds**() will be called in the **StartGame**() function just after the calls to **InitializeBubbles**(), **InitializeShots**(), and **InitializeShip**().

Now that our sounds are ready, we need to call the **Play**() function at the right time for each sound. We will show how to play the ship's acceleration sound here, and then you will complete the remaining sounds in the next activity!

We want the ship's acceleration sound to be played whenever the user accelerates the ship forward. In our Bubble Blaster game, the ship accelerates whenever the user presses the up arrow key. We examine each of the keys that are currently pressed in the **ProcessKeys**() method called by the timer event. We want our sound to play whenever the ship is accelerated, so the **ProcessKeys**() method is a great place to play the sound if the up arrow key is pressed.

Find your **ProcessKeys**() function and add a call to **accelerateSound.Play**() like this:

```
If (keyUpPressed) Then
    myShip.Accelerate(SHIP_ACCELERATION)
    accelerateSound.Play()  'play the acceleration sound
End If
```

 Now when you build and run the game you should hear the acceleration sound each time you move around the screen!

Chapter Review

- The simplest form of sound in a game is the beep.

- The beep sound was the only sound that original computer games could play.

- By changing the frequency and duration of a beep, you can completely change the sound it makes.

- The **Beep()** function makes a beep sound through the sound card. The **Console.Beep()** makes a sound through the PC speaker.

- The sound made by **Console.Beep()** can be changed by altering the frequency and duration.

- The invention of sound cards for computer meant you could play more complex sounds and music.

- Visual Basic can easily play uncompressed sounds from WAV files.

- The sound functions in Visual Basic require the "System.Media" library.

- A **SoundPlayer** control is used to play WAV files.

- Adding sounds as resources in your project will allow the sound to be referenced by **My.Resources** name instead of file path on your hard drive.

- You can play pre-defined Windows system sounds using the **SystemSound** object.

Your Turn! Finish Bubble Blaster Sounds

In this activity, you will add the last three sound effects to complete the Bubble Blaster game. This is the final code that you will add to the Bubble Blaster project that we have been working on for the past couple of chapters! Start up Visual Basic 2010 Express and open your Bubble Blaster project.

Exploding Bubbles

Add an explosion sound every time a bubble "explodes" on the screen. The **SoundPlayer** variable has already been created for this sound and initialized in the **InitializeSound**() function.

The explosion sound should be played every time a missile hits a bubble. In your program, you completed a function called **CheckShotCollisions**(), which finds when an bubble has been hit by a shot. This is a great place to play your explosion sound. Call **explodeSound.Play**()if a bubble has collided with a ship shot.

Ship Shots

The next sound is the shot sound. You want this sound to play whenever the space ship shoots a missile at a bubble. The ship shoots missiles whenever the user presses the spacebar key. The actual shot is launched from the **Shoot**() function which you completed in an earlier lesson. Add a call to **shotSound.Play**() whenever you find and initialize an unused shot in the **Shoot**() function.

Game Over

The last sound we will play when the space ship is destroyed by a bubble. In Bubble Blaster, we check to see if the ship has been hit in the function called **CheckShipCollisions**(). This is a good place to play our ship-destroyed sound. Make a call to **gameOverSound.Play**() whenever you determine your ship was destroyed.

 **Once you have all of your sounds in your program, give it a try! You'll see that with a little effort, adding sounds to a game can make a big difference!**

Once you have all of your sounds in your program, give it a try! You'll see that with a little effort, adding sounds to a game can make a big difference! You don't have to stick with the WAV files provided by the course! You can experiment with different WAV files to change your game play experience.

Chapter Ten: Artificial Intelligence

In this chapter we will discuss artificial intelligence, or AI. Computer games use artificial intelligence to provide computer opponents in games that may need more than one player or to make objects behave in a lifelike manner.

Lesson One: Understanding AI

Artificial intelligence is a favorite topic of Hollywood movies. The racks at the local video store are full of stories of robots with human-like intelligence and emotions. These creatures can constantly plan and adapt their goals and objectives. In reality, however, this type of AI does not exist. The human mind is the most powerful computer in the known universe! We have the amazing ability to understand and react to our surroundings, adjusting and adapting with ease. Modern machines are much more powerful than the earliest computers, but they are no match for the human brain.

The artificial intelligence that we will discuss in this lesson is not the Hollywood AI; it is the more realistic and simplistic intelligence that occurs in a typical computer game. Here are some examples of things you can do with AI in computer games:

- Control an opposing race car in a driving game
- Provide a computer opponent in a chess game
- Give lifelike behavior to non-playing-characters (NPCs) in a role playing game
- Control a bird's flight pattern and behavior as part of background scenery

These types of AI are limited to a narrow set of rules that may simulate lifelike behavior to some degree. More complex AI will result in a better simulation of real behavior, while very simple AI can result in more "robotic" or predictable behavior.

Go Fish

In this chapter we will use a version of the card game "Go Fish" to teach the creation of a simple artificial intelligence to control the computer opponent.

Go Fish is a popular card game for two players. When the game begins, each player is dealt 7 cards, face-down, from a deck of playing cards. The rest of the cards are placed face-down between the players. The object of the game is to get rid of all of the cards in your hand by making matches (sometimes called "books") of four of the same kind. For example, you can make a match of four Ace cards, or four King cards. To get these matches, each player will take turns asking the other player if they have a certain card. You must have at least one of the cards that you are asking for. You cannot ask for 2s if you do not have any 2s in your hand. If your opponent has any of the cards that you ask for, he or she must give you all of them. If your opponent does not have any of the cards that you have asked for, you must "Go Fish", or take one card from the deck. When you have four of a kind, you show the cards to your opponent and then place them face down next to you.

In our version of Go Fish, there will be one human player and one computer player. We have already written the basic Go Fish game. You will be writing the AI for the computer player!

Here is what the Go Fish game looks like:

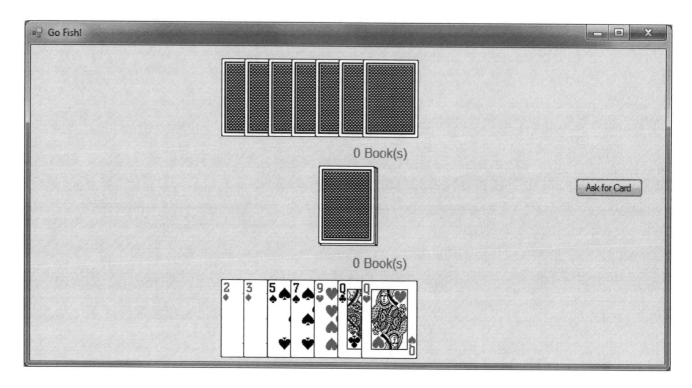

The human player's hand is shown at the bottom. The computer player's hand is at the top. The draw deck is in the middle, and each player's current score is shown in red. When it is the human's turn, click on one of your visible cards to select it, and then click the "Ask for Card" button to ask the opponent for those cards.

Lesson Two: Learning How to Fish

In this lesson we will develop a simple artificial intelligence needed to play the Go Fish game. The starter game provided for you has all of the game state, game logic, graphics, and other details already written for you -- but the computer does not yet know how to play!

So how do we teach a computer to play this game? First, think about how you would play the game yourself! What steps would you take when it becomes your turn? What cards would you be most likely to ask for? What game information would you need to remember about what has been going on in the game so far? What do you know about the cards in your opponent's hand? The end result of the AI function will be the selection of a card to ask for!

Now that we have the general idea, let's make a list of steps that will help decide which card to ask for.

Step One: The first thing we need to do is check if we have any cards in our hand. We can't ask for any cards if we don't have any in our hand. If we do not have any cards in our hand, then we will have to Go Fish!

Step Two: If we have one or more cards in our hand, then we need to select which one to ask for. The method we use to select a card may be very simple or more complex depending on how smartly we want the computer opponent to play.

The DoAI() Function

You are going to create all of the artificial intelligence for the computer player within the **DoAI**() function. This function needs to look at the game state to determine which card to pick and return an integer that specifies the selected card. If no card can be picked (because there are no cards in the computer's hand) then the function must return a constant called **NO_CARD_SELECTED**, which is already defined in the code.

```
Private Function DoAI() As Integer
End Sub
```

Often when designing some logic within a program it's useful to visualize the sequence of steps in a picture called a *flowchart*. A flowchart is a visual chart that can be used to describe a process. We will use two different shapes in our flowchart: a rectangle to represent an action and a diamond to represent a question or a decision that we have to make. Arrows connecting the shapes will indicate the program flow.

Let's start by creating a simple flowchart of what we know the **DoAI**() function has to do:

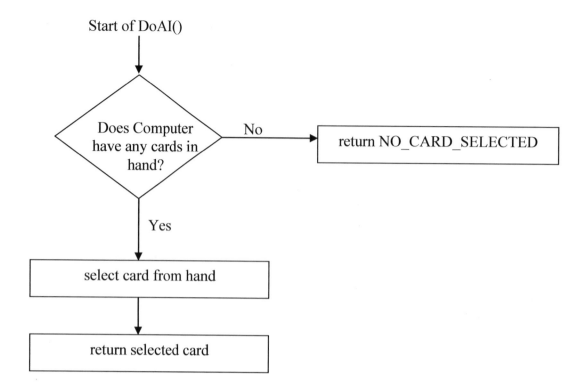

We can see from the flowchart there are two main things we need to do:

- Determine if the computer has any cards in hand
- Select a card to ask for from the hand

In order to finish these tasks you'll have to know a bit more about the Go Fish game state which contains information on all of the cards in the deck and which player they belong to, if any.

Go Fish Game State

In order to write the artificial intelligence functions you will need to understand how the Go Fish game tracks information in the game state. For starters, all game information is kept in a structure called **GameState** that is held in a variable called **myGameState**.

```
Private Structure GameState
    Dim deckOfCards() As Card
    ' there are some other Game State data elements we won't worry
    ' about now -- not necessary for the DoAI() method!
End Structure


Dim myGameState As GameState
```

The first and most important piece of information in this structure is the **deckOfCards** array. This array holds the card information for all 52 cards in the deck. Each card is represented by a **Card** data structure which contains information about each card:

```
Private Structure Card
    Dim isInBook As Boolean
    Dim currentPlayer As PlayerType
    Dim cardName As String

    ' there are some other Game State data elements we won't worry
    ' about now -- not necessary for the DoAI() method!
End Structure
```

The most important elements in the **Card** structure for our **DoAI()** function are:

isInBook	This **Boolean** will be **True** if the card has already been put into a matched book by some player or **False** if it is not yet in a book.
currentPlayer	This variable will show which player currently owns the card, either in the hand or already in a book. **PlayerType** is an object that we have created with three possible values: • PlayerType.NONE • PlayerType.COMPUTER • PlayerType.HUMAN.
cardName	The name of the card, not including suit. For instance, "Ace", "Queen", "10", "4", or "2".

Now that we have enough information about the game state, let's look at the main tasks we need to perform in the **DoAI()** function.

Designing the DoAI() Function

Remember that the two main tasks of the **DoAI()** function are:

- Determine if the computer has any cards in hand
- Select a card to ask for from the hand

For the first task, we know that all card information is stored in the **deckOfCards** array, and that each Card contains elements indicating which player (if any) owns the card and if the card is already in a book. You can probably imagine a function that will loop over the **deckOfCards** array and count the number of cards where **currentPlayer** is equal to **PlayerType.COMPUTER** and the **isInBook** value is **False**.

Fortunately, we needed this exact function elsewhere in the game logic, so we have pre-written it for you!

```
Private Function GetNumberOfCardsInHand(ByVal player As PlayerType) As Integer
```

All you have to do is call it for yourself, for example:

```
Dim numCardsInHand As Integer = GetNumberOfCardsInHand(PlayerType.COMPUTER)
```

You are going to create the card selection task all on your own, based on the information you know about the game state! For starters let's create a very simple method that simply selects a random card from the computer's hand. That's not very smart if you are a real person! But the logic is perfectly within the rules of the game and actually gives an "ok" simulation of a human opponent.

Let's revisit our flowchart and add more details based on what we now know will happen within our **DoAI()** function. This shows the overall flow of the logic you will write in the next activity!

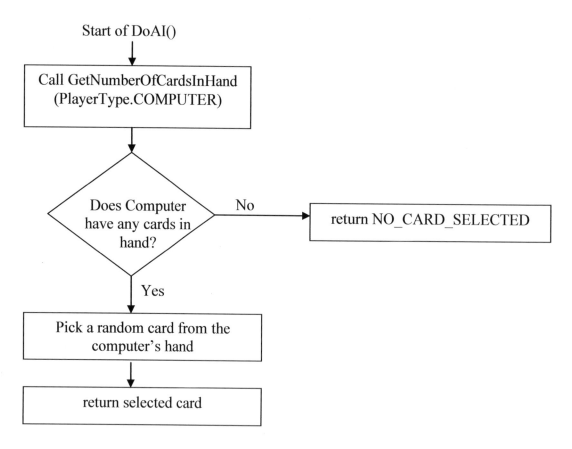

How do we identify a "selected" card? We will use the index of the card within the **deckOfCards** array! So if you want to select the first card in the array, the return value would be "0". If you want to select the last card in the array, the return value would be "51".

Your Turn! Completing the DoAI() Function

In this activity, you will implement the **DoAI()** function in order to provide some simple artificial intelligence for the Go Fish program. The goal of **DoAI()** is to select a card from the computer player's hand -- this is the card the computer player will ask the human player for during the computer's turn.

The starter project for this activity can be found in your "**\KidCoder\Game Programming\Activity Starters\Go Fish**" directory. The name of the solution for this chapter is "**Go Fish.sln**". Go ahead and open up the Visual Basic 2010 Express software and load this solution.

Find the **DoAI()** function you will complete. The function already contains the following pre-declared variables, which you can use in your loop that selects a random card.

```
Dim iRandomCard As Integer = NO_CARD_SELECTED
Dim isCardSelected As Boolean = False
```

First, see if the computer player has any cards in the hand by calling **GetNumberOfCardsInHand()** as described in the previous lesson. If there are no cards, you can just return the **NO_CARD_SELECTED** value.

If there are some cards in the computer's hand you will need to select a random card. The return value you produce will be the index into the **deckOfCards** array for the selected card.

To pick a random card from the computer hand, you can implement a simple **Do While** loop:

1. First, create a loop that continues until a valid card has been found.

```
Do While (isCardSelected = False)
```

2. Next, generate a random number from 0 up through 51 (these are valid indexes into our **deckOfCards** array). To pick a random number, use the random number generator called **myRandomGenerator** that is already created for you.) In effect, this is like picking a random card from the 52 cards in the deck. This statement will return a random value from 0 through 51:

```
iRandomCard = myRandomGenerator.Next(0, 52)
```

You can then access the random card with the phrase "**myGameState.deckOfCards(iRandomCard)**".

3. Create an **If** statement to see if this random card is the one you want to select. If the random card you picked is both owned by the computer and is not yet in a book, then you have found a valid random card in the computer's hand! Set the **isCardSelected** variable to **True** in order to exit from your loop. Hint: You will be checking the **iCurrentPlayer** and **isInBook** properties of your random card! Don't forget that the computer player is represented by **PLAYER_TYPE.COMPUTER**.

4. If the random card does not belong to the computer or it has already been placed in a book, just return to the beginning of the loop and try again with a new random number. You know that there is at least one valid card in the computer's hand, so eventually the random number will be a valid card index.

5. When you finally exit your **While** loop, the **iRandomCard** variable will contain the index of the card you want to select, so just **return** that value!

Now when you build and run Go Fish, you should have a computer opponent that plays against you!!

Lesson Three: Smarter Fisherman

In our last lesson we created a very simple artificial intelligence for the computer player in Go Fish. That AI works ok (at least it follows the rules of the game), but it's a little like playing against a toddler. The computer doesn't think very well, it just picks some card at random.

In this lesson we will discuss how to make our computer player a little smarter. You will put these thoughts into action when you create a better AI function in the next activity.

So what can our computer do to provide a more challenging opponent? Again, you want to think about what you would do when playing Go Fish yourself. Do you just pick a card at random in your hand and ask your opponent for it? Probably not! If you are a good player, you will keep track of what cards your opponent has asked for already, and if you ever draw that card yourself then you know what to ask for next!

For example, let's say that your opponent asks if you have any "4"s. You take a look at your hand, see that you do not have any "4"s and you smugly tell him (or her) to "Go Fish!" A couple of plays later, you have to "Go Fish" yourself and you pick up a "4" card from the deck. Now you have a plan! You know that your opponent must have some "4"s, since they have already asked for them. You wait for your turn and presto! You ask for "4"s and are rewarded with all of your opponent's "4" cards.

In your program, you can use the information in the Game State to keep track of what cards may be in the human player's hand. You don't want our computer player to cheat, so you cannot just scan the game state information to figure out what cards the human player has. Instead, you can create a separate array of card names to track which cards the human player has already asked for. Each time the human player asks for a card, you can add it to the array of cards you know the human player owns.

Let's take a look at the flowchart for a new **DoBetterAI**() method to implement this smarter logic:

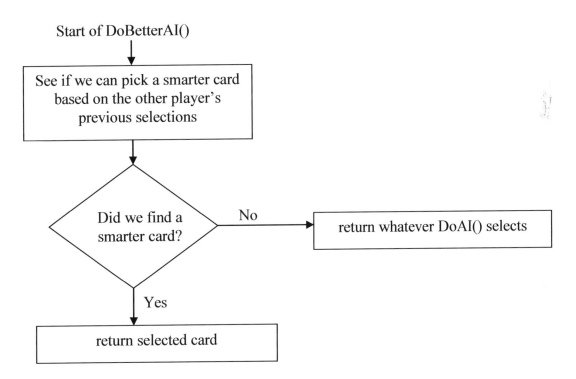

Our method for this advanced intelligence is still fairly simple. Instead of just picking a random card in the computer hand, you will first check the cards in the computer's hand against the cards that you know the human player has already requested. If the computer has a card in hand that the human player has asked for in the past, then you want to select that card!

Now of course it's possible that none of the cards in the computer's hand have been asked for by the human player. In this case, we can just fall back and pick a card at random using the existing **DoAI**() function that you created in the last lesson. After all, this is probably exactly what you would do if you were in that position!

Your Turn! Completing the Smarter Fisherman

In this activity, you will create a better version of AI for the computer player in our Go Fish game. This new intelligence will keep track of what cards the human player has asked for in the game. Since these are cards that you know are in the human's hand, you will ask for one of these cards first.

Go ahead and run the Microsoft Visual Basic 2010 Express software and open the Go Fish project that you worked on in the last lesson. Your **DoAI()** function should already be written and working!

First let's review an additional piece of the **GameState** structure that we skipped over earlier:

```
Private Structure GameState
    ' there are some other elements we've already described or that aren't
    ' interesting for artificial intelligence purposes
    Dim humansCards() As String
End Structure
```

The game state contains an array of strings called **humansCards**. This array contains the name of all cards the human player has previously asked for ("Ace", "4", etc). We have implemented all of the tracking logic already so you don't have to complete that tedious chore. See the **TrackHumansCards()** method if you are curious how this works.

There are two other important functions already defined...one of which is completely written and the other you will finish for this activity

| **DoBetterAI** | Implements the flowchart shown in the previous lesson. **GetBetterCard()** is called first, and if that selects a smarter card then just return it. Otherwise calls the existing **DoAI()** method you implemented previously to select a random card. |
| **GetBetterCard** | This is the method you will implement to see if the computer player has a card in hand that matches one of the cards known to be in the human hand. |

Now you will need to fill in the **GetBetterCard()** function.

```
Private Function GetBetterCard() As Integer
End Sub
```

Just like **DoAI**(), this function must return an index of the selected card (0-51) or the value **NO_CARD_SELECTED** if no better card was found.

GetBetterCard() will compare the cards that the human player has asked for with the cards that are in the computer player's hand. If you find a match then return that computer player's card index as the selected card. If there is no match, then return **NO_CARD_SELECTED**.

The activity starter declares one variable at the top of this function:

```
Dim cardToAskFor As Integer = NO_CARD_SELECTED
```

This is the value that you will return at the end of your function. By default we set it to NO_CARD_SELECTED, and you will change this if you find a card to ask for!

To write **GetBetterCard**(), you should:

- Create a **For** loop that will loop through all 52 cards in the **deckOfCards** array.

```
For i = 0 To 51
```

  o In order to work with each card individually, we will declare a temporary **Card** variable called **thisCard**.

```
Dim thisCard As Card = myGameState.deckOfCards(i)
```

  o If the card belongs to the computer and is not in a book, then it is a card in the computer's hand, and we need to figure out if we want to ask for it based on what we know of the human's cards!
    - Create another **For** loop over all of the strings in the **myGameState.humanCards** array. Remember that the array will change size over time so loop based on the current length:

```
For j = 0 To myGameState.humansCards.Length - 1
```

      - For each card name in the **humansCards** array

- Check to see if the human's card name (**myGameState.humansCards(j)**) equals the computer player's card name (**thisCard.cardName**)
- If they are equal, then:
  - Set the **cardToAskFor** variable equal to the index (**i**) of the *outer* **For** loop (which represents the card we have chosen!)
  - Set the **myGameState.humanCards(j)** array string equal to "DELETED" which will keep it from causing a match again.

At the end of the function, return the current value of **cardToAskFor**. This may be **NO_CARD_SELECTED** if you couldn't find a smarter card or the card index of a card we know the human player has in their hand!

Now when you build and run Go Fish, the computer opponent should be a little bit tougher! The difference may not be obvious at first, but if you play enough games you should notice the computer player more often asking for cards that you have already shown to have in your hand.

Congratulations, you have now written your first game with AI! While your AI won't figure out how to take over the world any time soon, you now know the type of logic it takes to make multi-player games fun for only one person to play!

Chapter Review

- The artificial intelligence shown in Hollywood movies is not realistic for actual game programming.
- Computer games tend to use simple intelligence that fills one very narrow purpose such as making a computer opponent play according to the game rules with some degree of skill.
- Artificial intelligence can also be used to make objects or non-playing characters in the environment more lifelike.
- To create artificial intelligence for a computer player, you need to think of the steps that you would take to play the game.
- These steps are then turned into coded logic that allows the computer to "play" the game.
- You can use a flowchart to visualize the steps needed to write a function.
- AI algorithms can use the game state information to help make decisions
- More advanced AI allows for more lifelike actions from the computer.
- In order to avoid having the computer opponent cheat it may be necessary to build additional game state information that isn't directly used by the game rules. This extra information may show what the computer opponent "should" reasonably know if they were in fact a human opponent.

All of the Your Turn activities for this chapter have already been completed during the chapter lessons!

Chapter Eleven: Saving Your Games

In this chapter we will explore saving and loading your games. When your games become longer and more complex, your users will need a way to handle game interruptions. A user may even want to create a "checkpoint" in a game by saving their current position. Then if the game ends early, players can load their last position from disk instead of starting over at the beginning.

Lesson One: File Input and Output

In order to understand how to save a game, you will need to learn simple file operations in Visual Basic. Reading and writing to files is often referred to as file input and output or "File I/O". Visual Basic file I/O functions are kept in a library called "**System.IO**", so we will import this library at the top of every program that will read and write to files.

```
Imports System.IO
```

Now we can use all of the file functions in the **System.IO** library from within our program.

In order to save and load a game we need to be able to create files on the computer's hard disk that contain game state information, and then read those files back from disk to restore the game state information later.

File Extensions

A file *extension* is the last part of the filename after the period. You are probably already familiar with many different file extensions such as .EXE (executable program), .PDF (document), .WAV (audio file), and .JPG (image file).

We will be saving our games by writing certain information to a text file. This means that any file we create will be readable by programs like Windows Notepad, WordPad, or other text file editors. By storing our game information in text format you will be able to easily read the file to ensure the values are correct. Typically, a text file is given an extension of .TXT, but this is not required. You can create a text file with any name that you want, such as: .GAM, .FISH, .BOB, etc. As long as we are writing text strings to the file when it is created, we can still view it with Notepad or any other text file editor.

In fact, it is sometimes better to create a saved game file with a different extension than .TXT. Why? We don't really want anyone to change the text in a saved game file on their own. A file with an extension of

.TXT is easily opened by Windows because they are usually associated with Notepad, WordPad, or some other default text editor. All a user has to do is double-click on the file and voila! They are easily able to read and change the file contents. This could result in disaster when the game program tries to load this file to restore the game state. For this reason, we may want to disguise our text files as something else.

To disguise our text file, we will create a special extension for the file, like .GAM. We will still write text to the file, and it will still be a text file, but the user will not be able to open the file just by double-clicking on it. Can you still view the file in Notepad or some other text editor? Absolutely! Just run the Notepad program, tell it to open a file, choose *.* as the type of file and choose your .GAM file from the list of files on your hard drive:

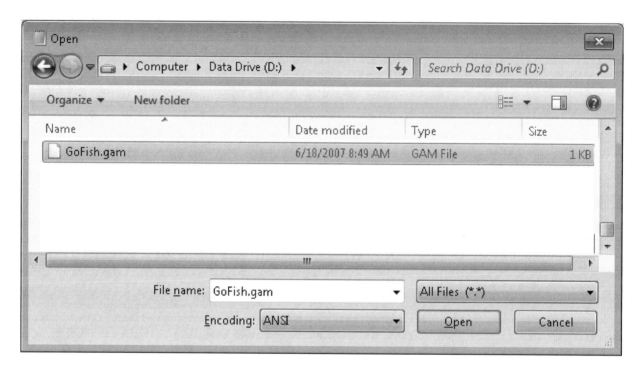

You will then be able to read and modify the text file contents.

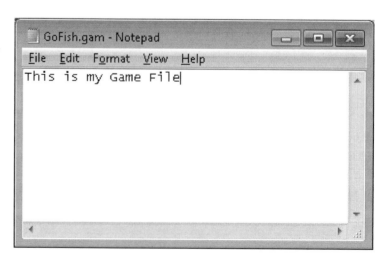

If our users see that a game's save file has a special extension such as .GAM, they will probably think it is some special, super-secret file that they should leave alone. They will never know it is a simple text file!

StreamWriter

To create our text file, we will use an object from the **System.IO** library called **StreamWriter**. A **StreamWriter** will allow us to open a file and then write lines of text to the file. A **StreamWriter** variable is declared like any other data type:

```
Dim myFileWriter As StreamWriter
```

Now we have to create a new **StreamWriter** object to store in the variable. The parameter to the new **StreamWriter** object is the name of the file we want to create:

```
myFileWriter = New StreamWriter("c:\myGame.gam")
```

This will create a file named "myGame.gam" in the "c:\ root" directory. You can also just use the filename such as "myGame.gam" and the file will be saved to wherever the program is currently running. In the next lesson, we will take a look at a way to allow the user to choose the file name and location.

Now that we have opened our file, let's write some text! The **StreamWriter.WriteLine()** function will write a single line of text to a file:

```
myFileWriter.WriteLine( "Game Information")
```

We can use one **WriteLine()** statement for each line of text that we want to write to the file. Then when we are done, we just close the file to finish the process:

```
myFileWriter.Close()
```

That's really all there is to writing lines of text to a file: just four simple lines of code!

StreamReader

When we want to read a file back into our game, we use the same **System.IO** library. Instead of a **StreamWriter**, though, we will use a **StreamReader**. This object is declared just like a **StreamWriter**:

```
Dim myFileReader As StreamReader
```

Similarly, we have to create a new **StreamReader** object to store in the variable. The parameter to the new **StreamReader** object is the name of the file we want to read:

```
myFileReader = New StreamReader("c:\myGame.gam")
```

Now we are ready to read lines of text from our file. We will use the **StreamReader.ReadLine**() function, which will return a single line of text from a file:

```
Dim stringFromFile As String = myFileReader.ReadLine()
```

The statement above will place a line from our file into the **String** variable **stringFromFile**. If the file is empty, the value of **stringFromFile** will be a value called **Nothing**. **Nothing** is a special value in Visual Basic. A value of **Nothing** means that we did not retrieve any information at all. If **stringFromFile** is equal to **Nothing** after the **ReadLine()** function, then there is no more information in the file. Notice that the value **Nothing** and the string "Nothing" are two very different things!

Make sure you call **StreamReader.Close**() when done with the file, otherwise you may keep it open and prevent others from accessing it later!

Here is a longer example where we create a new file, write several lines of text, then read them back and print out the results for confirmation:

```
' open new file called myGame.gam
Dim myFileWriter As StreamWriter = New StreamWriter("myGame.gam")

' write out 4 lines of text
myFileWriter.WriteLine("Game Information")
myFileWriter.WriteLine("1")
myFileWriter.WriteLine("2")
myFileWriter.WriteLine("Kalamazoo")

' close the file
myFileWriter.Close()

' open existing file called myGame.gam
Dim myFileReader As StreamReader = New StreamReader("myGame.gam")

' create a variable to hold lines of text we read from a file
Dim myLine As String = Nothing

' loop over all lines of text in the file
Do
        ' read next line of text
        myLine = myFileReader.ReadLine()
```

```
         ' if we got something
     If (myLine <> Nothing) Then
         ' display line of text to the user
         MsgBox(myLine, MsgBoxStyle.OkOnly, "Line from file")
     End If

         ' loop until we got Nothing from the ReadLine() function
  Loop Until myLine = Nothing

myFileReader.Close()   ' tidy up the open file when we're done
```

If you type in and run this code sample then you will see a file called "myGame.gam" created in the directory next to your executable (.exe) program. You can edit the text file with Windows Notepad or any other text editor and see the lines

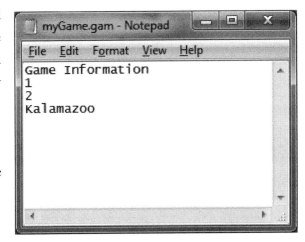

Those same lines of text should be displayed by the message box when the file is read back in the **Do** loop!

Lesson Two: SaveFileDialog and OpenFileDialog

In the last lesson, we talked about how to write and read information from a file. For all of the previous examples we used a specific filename directly entered into the code. This is not always ideal since it will only allow us to save one game at a time. What if we have a whole family of people who want to play our game? They would probably want to save their own games and make the filenames more meaningful like "jack.gam" or "susie.gam". In this lesson we will learn how the user can choose the file name and location for their saved game.

What we would like is a separate form or screen that allows the user to browse through their hard drive directory structure and choose the location and file name to use for the saved game. We could create that form ourselves, but it's quite a bit of effort! Fortunately Visual Basic already has a nice little control that will handle all of this for us!

Save File Dialog

The "Save As" dialog is a built-in screen that you can use to let a user select a target filename on their hard drive. Depending on your version of Windows the "Save As" dialog will look something like this:

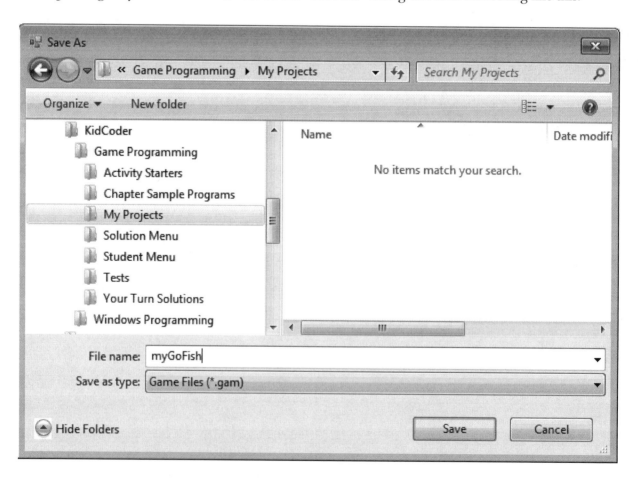

The user can click through the directory tree on the left, and select a target file on the right. They may also type in a new filename (such as "myGoFish") in the "File name" edit field. The extension type is controlled by the bottom combo box (e.g. "Game Files (*.gam)"). The user clicks the "Save" button when they have chosen the right file, or "Cancel" to avoid picking anything.

Look at the Visual Basic Toolbox from your form Design screen. You should see a group of controls called "Dialogs". Dialogs are pre-built screens that are used to do specific functions, like opening and saving files. In this group, there is a control named **SaveFileDialog**. If you add this to your form, the control will show up at the bottom of your design screen, as seen below.

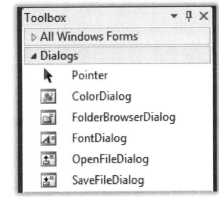

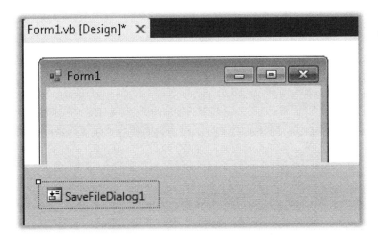

You then use that control variable (in our case "SaveFileDialog1") by name in your program code.

By default, if you do not set any properties of your dialog, the "Save as type" field will be empty:

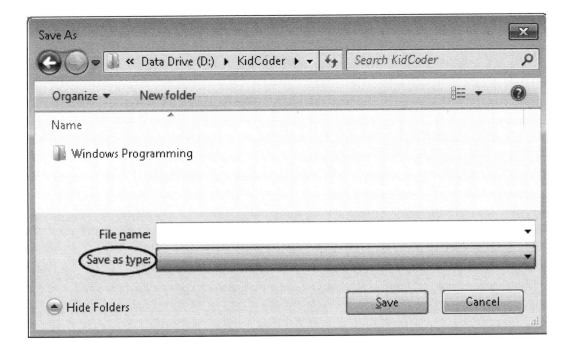

The "Save as type" field serves as a filter that only allows file names of certain extensions to be displayed in the dialog. For instance, if we only wanted to show ".gam" files, we can add that filter in the **SaveFileDialog**'s properties window. Right-click on the **SaveFileDialog1** control in your form and then look at the Properties window. You should see a property called **Filter**. Here is where we can tell the **SaveFileDialog** what files we want to show to the user.

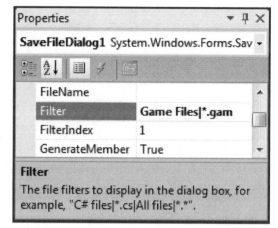

For our filter, we want to add the value:

"Game Files|*.gam"

This filter value will tell the dialog two things: First, it will add an item to the "Save as type" drop-down list box that says "Game Files". Second, we tell the dialog that the "Game Files" are the files that end with ".gam". These two items are separated with the bar character "|", which is located above the "\" character on your keyboard. If we wanted the user to choose other types of files, we could add items to the filter by adding more file types and extensions like this in the Filter field:

Game Files|*.gam|Text Files|*.txt|All Files|*.*

Now we have put three items in our "Save as type" drop down list box:

- "Game files", with an extension of "*.gam"
- "Text files", with an extension of "*.txt"
- "All Files", with any extension "*.*"

Now the "Save as type" combo box in our dialog would contain those three options:

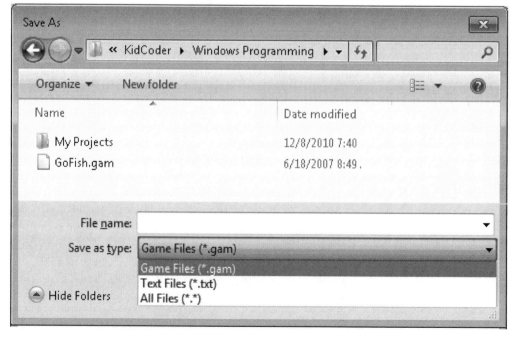

ShowDialog

In order to display the Save Dialog in the game, we need to call a function on our SaveFileDialog object called **ShowDialog**():

```
SaveFileDialog1.ShowDialog()
```

This will display our Save Dialog on the screen. Once you make the call to **ShowDialog**(), your program's control has been handed over to the Save Dialog window. The next statement in our program is not run until the user clicks either the "Save" or "Cancel" button on the **OpenFileDialog** window.

DialogResult

When the user clicks on either the "Save" or "Cancel" button on the Save Dialog screen, the dialog will send back some information in a variable called a **DialogResult**.

```
Dim results As DialogResult
```

You should save the return value from ShowDialog into this variable:

```
Dim results As DialogResult = SaveFileDialog1.ShowDialog()
```

This one line of code does several things! First, our game is paused and the Save Dialog is shown on the screen. When the user exits the Save Dialog (with either the "Save" or "Cancel" button), the **results** variable is given a value of **DialogResult.OK** or **DialogResult.Cancel** depending on what button the user pressed. We can then check the value and decide what to do next in the game program.

If the return value is **DialogResult.Cancel**, then the user must have clicked the "Cancel" button. In this case, you don't want to do anything since the user has changed their mind about saving their game.

If the return value is **DialogResult.OK**, then the user has clicked the "Save" button and we can continue with saving their game information.

FileName

If we will be saving their game information, then we will need to know what file was chosen in the Save Dialog. The file that the user selected to save their information is held in a property of the Save Dialog control called **FileName**. We can then use this value to create a **StreamWriter** and write our information to the user's file.

Here is a full code example that shows the dialog, checks the result, and creates a **StreamWriter** using the filename selected by the user.

```
Dim results As DialogResult = SaveFileDialog1.ShowDialog()
If (results = DialogResult.OK) Then
        ' open new file using the FileName property from the SaveFileDialog
        Dim myFileWriter As StreamWriter = _
                    New StreamWriter(SaveFileDialog1.FileName)
        ' continue writing to your file as in the previous example...

Else
        ' Code to be run if Cancel button was clicked
End If
```

Open File Dialog

When the user is ready to load a saved game back from disk we would like for them to pick the file to load. Fortunately we can use another control called the **OpenFileDialog** control to let the user pick the filename. The **OpenFileDialog** control can be found in the Toolbox, near the **SaveFileDialog** control. If you add this to your form, the control will show up at the bottom of your design screen, just like the **SaveFileDialog** control. You can then access the **OpenFileDialog** variable from your code.

The Open File screen looks similar to the Save File dialog:

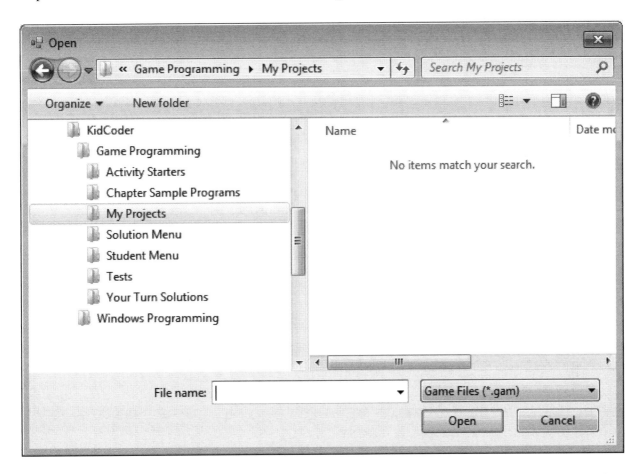

The user picks their target filename and then clicks "Open" or "Cancel". The combo box in the lower right contains the file type filter.

You can filter the filenames that are shown to the user in the **OpenFileDialog** just like the **SaveFileDialog**. If you click on the **OpenFileDialog** object on your form and then look at the properties sheet, you will see the **Filter** property. This Filter works exactly like the Filter property for the **SaveFileDialog**, so we can add the following to the Filter to only display saved files of type ".gam":

"Game Files|*.gam"

Adding a filter to select our game files is very important, since we want to make sure that our program is going to try and load information from the correct file type. If the user picked some other file type (such as an executable file (.EXE), a document (.PDF), or an image file) our program would certainly now know how to read it!

Using **OpenFileDialog** is almost identical to **SaveFileDialog**. Call the **ShowDialog()** method to display the Open Dialog and then check the results to see if they hit the "Open" or "Cancel" button. Once you get an OK result, you can read the **OpenFileDialog**.**FileName** property to get the file name chosen by the user.

This code sample shows how to declare a **DialogResult** variable, display the dialog, check the result, and open a **StreamReader** on the selected filename.

```
Dim results As DialogResult = OpenFileDialog1.ShowDialog()
If (results = DialogResult.OK) Then
        ' open existing file called myGame.gam
        Dim myFileReader As StreamReader =
                New StreamReader(OpenFileDialog1.FileName)
        ' continue reading file as specified in the previous example
Else
        'Code to be executed if Cancel button was clicked
End If
```

That's all the file handling skills you need to load and save a game! You now know how to create new files and write out some data, how to open existing files to read in data, and how to let the user conveniently choose the file names for the load and save operations within the game.

Next you'll learn how to actually convert your game state to lines of text to be written to your file, and how to load lines of text back into your game state when needed!

Lesson Three: Saving and Loading the Game State

In our last lessons, we learned how to save and load data from files and how to use the **OpenFileDialog** and the **SaveFileDialog** controls. But what information do we need to keep in order "save" a user's place in the game? If we were to "freeze" a game right now, what information would we need to re-create the game later? The answers to these questions really depend on the game that we are trying to save.

To figure out what information should be saved for your game, ask yourself some questions like these:

- If this is a multi-player game, who is the current player?
- What is the current score and level of the game?
- Are there any elements of the game that belong to specific players?
- Are the current positions of the players important?
- What sprites do I have, and what are their positions, angles, speeds, and images?

If you have planned and designed your game carefully, all of this information will be found in one central location: the game state. Your game state should be a nicely defined structure or set of variables that keeps track of all the goings-on in your game. However this doesn't mean you need to save every piece of information in your game state to a file! Instead, take a look at the information in your game state and figure out what minimum information is necessary to re-create the game at a later time.

For example, you would definitely need to know who the current player is, but you might not need to know their exact location on the screen. If we were saving the Bubble Blaster game, it would be appropriate to save the number and size of the Bubbles left on the screen and probably the current location, direction, and speed of all the objects. But you can probably ignore any shots that happen to be fired on the screen at the time the game was saved. When the game is reloaded just assume that no shots have been fired. Making decisions about what information is crucial and what information can be ignored may save time and effort when we saving and loading the game.

SaveGame()

Once you have identified the information that needs to be saved, you will need to create a function in your program that will gather the information and write it to a file. You can name this function anything you would like, but a name like **SaveGame()** probably makes the most sense. What needs to happen within a **SaveGame()** function? The details will vary from game to game, but in general these steps should be taken:

- Get the user's filename using the **SaveFileDialog**
- Create the file with **StreamWriter**
- Write all relevant game state information to the file
- Close the **StreamWriter** file

How exactly will you write out the selected variables from the game state? Remember that we are writing a text file, so you will want to convert all of the variables that are not already string to a string format. Usually this is pretty easy. When you have your strings then just write out one variable per line and, most importantly, remember the order of the variables so you can load them back correctly later! If you have an array, then write out the array elements from within a loop, one element at a time. What if the array has a variable size? Then you will want to write the size of the array out first so you know how many elements to read back in later!

While this sounds easy, it can take a bit of practice to make it all work smoothly. We'll walk you through an example in this chapter's activity!

LoadGame()

How will the user re-open their game and start playing again? We will need another function added to the game which will re-populate the game state from the saved game file and re-start the game. You can name this function anything you want, but we'll use **LoadGame()**.

To load the saved game you'll need to take these general steps from within **LoadGame()**:

- Get the target filename using the **OpenFileDialog**.
- Open the file with **StreamReader**
- Read all relevant game state information from the file into your game state
- Close the **StreamReader** file
- Take any other necessary action to cause the game to start using the newly loaded game state (for instance, redraw the screen or restart a timer).

LoadGame() is, unsurprisingly, just the reverse of **SaveGame()**. How do you know the order and type of variables that are stored in the saved file? By looking at the **SaveGame()** method! You need to read the variables back in exactly the same order that they were written out. Remember that all variables will be read back as strings, but you may need to convert them to **Integers**, **Boolean**, or other data types.

If you have saved an array in the file you will need to **ReDim** your array variable to match the new array length. If the length is not a fixed value known in advance (e.g. 52 cards) then you should have written out the array length before to the array data. Then you can read the array length first, **ReDim** the game state array to the correct length, and loop the correct number of times reading in the array data.

Again, while sounding easy, this is best learned by doing an actual example! The chapter activity will guide you through both saving and loading a game state.

Chapter Review

- File I/O stands for file input and output.

- Visual Basic file functions are kept in the **System.IO** library.

- A file extension is the group of letters that occur after the period in a filename.

- A file's extension is often used in Windows to determine what program will be used to open the file.

- It is sometimes better to create a game file that has an unusual file extension. This keeps curious users from accidentally opening and damaging the game file.

- A **StreamWriter** object is used to write data to a file.

- The **StreamWriter.WriteLine()** function is used to write a line of data to a file.

- A **StreamReader** object is used to read data from a file.

- The **StreamReader.ReadLine()** function is used to read a line of data from a file.

- There are two helper dialogs in the Visual Basic toolbox: the **SaveFileDialog** and the **OpenFileDialog**.

- These dialogs allow a user to pick files to open or save with a common look and feel.

- The **Filter** property for these dialogs will allow the programmer to determine what file extensions to allow the user to open or save.

- Read the **FileName** property from the dialog variable to find out what file the user selected.

- In order to save a game's state, you must decide what information is needed to re-create it later on.

- Create your own **SaveGame()** and **LoadGame()** methods that work together to save and load your game state.

Your Turn! Freezing and Thawing Fish

In this activity you will add the ability to save and load games in your Go Fish program. Open the Visual Basic 2010 Express software and load the Go Fish project that you worked on in the last chapter.

The activity starter already contains buttons to save and load the game, but they have been hidden so far! Your first order of business is to make these buttons visible so the user can click them. In the form design window, change the **Visible** property for the **SaveButton** and the **LoadButton** to **True**. This will make these buttons appear on the screen when the user starts up the game.

The following four functions have been pre-defined in Go Fish to support the saving and loading of games.

SaveButton_Click	**SaveButton** event handler function; calls **SaveGame**().
LoadButton_Click	**LoadButton** event handler function; calls **LoadGame**() and repaints the screen.
SaveGame	Save the current game state to a file specified by the user
LoadGame	Loads the current game state from a file specified by the user

The two click methods have already been finished for you, but **SaveGame()** and **LoadGame()** are empty; these are your responsibility!

Important Game State Information

The Go Fish game state structure contains the following elements:

```
Private Structure GameState
    Dim deckOfCards() As Card

    Dim iCurrentPlayer As Integer
    Dim iCurrentCardSelected As Integer
    Dim iNumComputerBooks As Integer
    Dim iNumHumanBooks As Integer
    Dim gameOver As Boolean
    Dim cardsInDeck As Integer

    Dim humansCards() As String
End Structure
```

In order to successfully restore a Go Fish game you will need to save the following elements:

deckOfCards	Each **Card** element is a structure full of data. But all you need to save from each Card is the **currentPlayer** and **isInBook**. All others do not change during the game.
iCurrentPlayer	We need to know which player has the current turn after loading the game
iNumComputerBooks	We should keep track of the computer's score!
iNumHumanBooks	We should also keep track of the human player's score!
iCardsInDeck	Save and load this variable too, which is used in several places.

We will ignore the **humansCards** used by the artificial intelligence for simplicity, and the other elements (**iCurrentCardSelected** and **gameOver**) can be ignored as well.

SaveGame()

To implement your **SaveGame()** method complete these steps on the Form design screen:

- Add a **SaveFileDialog** control to the form (you can leave the name of the control as **SaveFileDialog1**).
- Change the **Filter** property to only accept *.gam files.

Then, find the empty **SaveGame()** method and implement the following logic:

```
Private Sub SaveGame()
End Sub
```

- Create a variable named **FileWriter** as type **StreamWriter**.
- Create variable named **results** as type **DialogResult**.
- Call the **ShowDialog()** function on the **SaveFileDialog** control. Set the **results** variable equal to the return value of this function.
- If the **results** variable equals **DialogResult.OK**
  - Set the **FileWriter** equal to a **New StreamWriter** object with the **SaveFileDialog1.FileName**. This will create a new file with that name.

```
FileWriter = New StreamWriter(SaveFileDialog1.FileName)
```

  - Now you need to loop through the **myGameState.deckOfCards** array and do the following for each card in the array:

179

- Use two **WriteLine()** functions for the **FileWriter** to write the following information to the file:
  - The **currentPlayer** value for each card.
  - The **isInBook** value for each card.
- After you have looped through the entire deck, you will need to save the other remaining game state variables we specified earlier, again using a **WriteLine()** function call for each piece of information (located in **myGameState**):
  - The **iCurrentPlayer** in the game.
  - The number of books (**iNumComputerBooks**) that the computer has made.
  - The number of books (**iNumHumanBooks**) that the human player has made.
  - The number of cards (**iCardsInDeck**) left in the deck.
  - Finally, you can close the file by calling the StreamWriter's **Close()** function.
- If the **results** variable did not return **DialogResult.OK** (the user hit the "Cancel" button on the **SaveFileDialog** screen), send a **MsgBox** to the user telling them the game was not saved.

 Now when you build and run your program you should see the Load and Save buttons. The Load button won't do anything yet, but your Save button should let you save your game! After your ".gam" file is created you can look at it in Windows Notepad or other text editor to see the contents of all the variables you saved.

LoadGame()

To implement your **LoadGame()** method you will want to complete these steps on the Form design screen:

- Add an **OpenFileDialog** control to the form.
- Change the **Filter** property to only accept *.gam files.

Then, find the empty **LoadGame()** method and implement the following logic:

```
Private Sub LoadGame()
End Sub
```

- Create a variable named **FileReader** as type **StreamReader**.
- Create variable named **results** as type **DialogResult**.
- Set the **OpenFileDialog1.Filename** property to an empty string "".

- Call the **ShowDialog**() function on the **OpenFileDialog** control. Set the `results` variable equal to the return value of this function.

- If the `results` variable equals **DialogResult.OK**
  - Set the **FileReader** equal to a **New StreamReader** object with the **OpenFileDialog1.FileName.** This will create a new file with that name.

```
FileReader = New StreamReader(OpenFileDialog1.FileName)
```

  - Now you need to loop through the **myGameState.deckOfCards** array and do the following for each card in the array:
    - Use two **ReadLine**() functions for the **FileReader** to read the following information from the file into the current card in the array:
      - The **currentPlayer** value for each card.
      - The **isInBook** value for each card.
    - **If** the card's **currentPlayer** is **PlayerType.NONE** then you need to set the card sprite's **IsAlive** property to **False.** Otherwise a non-owned card may lurk around "alive" in the background behind other cards and confuse the game!
    - **Else If** the card is not in a book, then it is in a player's hand, so set the sprite's **IsAlive** property to **True** to make sure it is visible!

  - After you have looped through the entire deck, you will need to load the other remaining game state variables we specified earlier, again using a **ReadLine**() function call for each piece of information (located in **myGameState**):
    - The **iCurrentPlayer** in the game.
    - The number of books (**iNumComputerBooks**) that the computer has made.
    - The number of books (**iNumHumanBooks**) that the human player has made.
    - The number of cards (**iCardsInDeck**) left in the deck.

  - Call **FileReader.Close**() when you are done reading the file!

- If the `results` variable did not return **DialogResult.OK** (the user hit the "Cancel" button on the **OpenFileDialog** screen), send a **MsgBox** to the user telling them the game was not loaded.

That's it! The existing **LoadButton_Click()** function will call **DisplayHand**() for the computer and human players to repaint the screen after the saved game is loaded.

You are ready to fully test your program and see if you can freeze and thaw your fish! The Load button will let you pick a ".gam" file and your previous game is then automatically loaded. You should be able to continue playing from where you left off originally.

Chapter Twelve: Game Physics

As you move sprites around in a game environment they may encounter collisions or other forces that, in real life, should make them bounce or move in a certain way. In order to make the movement of your sprites believable, they should follow the same rules of physics that exist in the real world. When you throw something into the "air" in your program, it should act as if gravity is pulling it back down to the ground. When you bounce an object against a wall, it should bounce back in a realistic manner. The term *game physics* is used to describe the set of rules applied to your objects that make them behave (at least to some degree) according to the laws of physics.

This chapter will describe how to make your sprites move in a manner similar to real-world objects that bounce off a flat surface or are thrown or shot into the air.

Lesson One: Reflection

We typically think of reflection when we look at our image in the mirror, or in a calm lake on a sunny day. What we see in those cases is the reflection of light bouncing off of a surface and reflecting back at us. A ball that hits a flat surface will reflect in exactly the same way. We use the term "reflection" to describe what happens to the direction of the object while bouncing off a flat surface.

If you have ever bounced a ball off of the ground, you know the angle at which you throw the ball determines the direction it will bounce. If you throw it straight down it will bounce straight up. If you throw it at a large angle it will bounce at a large angle.

The angle of the reflection is determined by a law of physics called the "Law of Reflection". This law says that any object that hits a flat surface at an angle will be reflected off of the flat surface at that same angle on the other side of a perpendicular (straight intersection) line. This is demonstrated in the picture to the right.

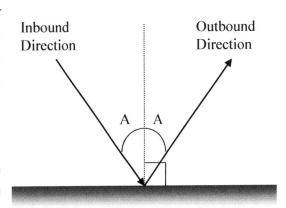

The angle "A" the incoming object makes with the perpendicular line will be matched by the same angle "A" on the other side as the object leaves in the outbound direction.

You used reflection in the last course when we created the Pong program. The Pong ball would bounce (or reflect) off of the top and sides of the screen according to the law of reflection, even though we didn't explain the physics behind the behavior at the time!

The method for creating reflection off a straight horizontal or vertical line in a game is simple. To reflect an object off any vertical line (such as the left or right side of the screen) just reverse the X direction of the object! Simply multiply the X direction with negative 1. To reflect an object off any horizontal line (such as the top or bottom of the screen) just reverse the Y direction of the object. Again, this can be done by multiplying the Y direction with negative 1.

The following example demonstrates reflecting off a vertical and horizontal line (assuming **mySprite** has been previously declared as a **Sprite** from our Sprite Library):

```
' to bounce off a vertical line, reverse the X direction
mySprite.Velocity.X = mySprite.Velocity.X * -1

' to bounce off a horizontal line, reverse the Y direction
mySprite.Velocity.Y = mySprite.Velocity.Y * -1
```

Notice that we are just changing the direction of the object, but not the speed. The sprite will only move faster or slower if you increase or decrease the magnitude of the X or Y velocity components. But just changing the sign of the X or Y components will make it move at the same speed in a different direction!

Lesson Two: Gravity and Projectiles

Many computer games involve the use of objects that are either thrown or shot into the air. In the real world, every object that is launched or thrown into the air is influenced by the force of gravity. The Earth's gravity is a force which is constantly pulling everything towards the center of the earth (or, in terms of the computer screen, straight down).

When you throw a ball into the air, it will travel up and away from you. As soon as it leaves your hands, gravity begins to work on the ball. Depending on how hard you throw, the ball will eventually stop going in the upwards direction and will start moving down towards the ground. The arc that the ball follows from the time you throw it until the time it hits the ground is called a parabolic arc, which is shaped like an upside-down "U".

Let's take a look at a diagram that shows a ball moving under the force of gravity on the screen:

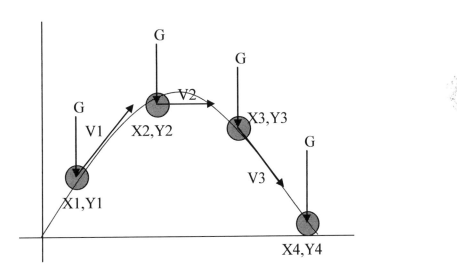

The original position of the ball is shown as point (X1, Y1). The ball has an initial velocity of V1, which is moving the ball in the negative Y direction (up), and positive X direction (to the right). We also have the force of gravity "G", which is pushing down on the ball. The effect is to reduce the negative velocity in the Y direction and leave the X velocity untouched.

The next position, point (X2, Y2), shows where the ball is a short time later. Here, gravity has slowed the Y direction movement to zero, and our ball is only moving in the positive X direction (to the right).

The next position, point (X3, Y3) again shows the position of the ball after another short time. Now, gravity has reversed the Y direction so that the direction is now positive (moving down on the screen). Finally, we see the last position of the ball (X4, Y4) which shows the ball where it has landed on the "ground".

The dotted parabolic line in the diagram shows how the ball would move in the real world. Notice that the speed of the ball from left to right in the X direction is completely unaffected by the force of gravity. Gravity only acts to change the velocity in the Y direction. Also notice that the force of gravity "G" is a constant that affects the ball equally at each position. In terms of our **Sprite** Library, gravity is an acceleration applied at every timer tick that only affects the Y direction!

You are already familiar with one **Sprite** Library acceleration function from the Bubble Blaster game. The ship in this game can accelerate in whatever direction that it is pointing and the ship's speed and position will be updated accordingly. A second **Sprite.Acceleration()** function allows you to apply an acceleration in the X and Y directions separately, regardless of what direction the sprite is currently traveling.

```
Public Sub Accelerate(ByVal AX As Double, ByVal AY As Double)
```

The AX parameter represents the acceleration (or, if negative, the deceleration) of the X speed. The AY parameter represents the acceleration (or, if negative, the deceleration) of the Y speed. We know that gravity only affects the speed of the Y component of an object. When using this function to apply gravity, set the AX parameter to zero. Then set the value of the AY parameter to represent gravity. For example:

```
mySprite.Accelerate(0.0, 0.04)
```

You'll have to play with several different values to find a value for the strength of gravity that "feels" right for your game environment. The size of the AY parameter will determine how quickly the object will fall back down to the ground. Remember that in computer terms, an object moving "down" has a positive Y speed, so a positive Y acceleration will end to speed up an object's fall down the screen.

Sprite.Move() Function

In earlier games when a sprite moved off the edge of the screen, we merely wrapped it to the other side using the **MoveAndWrap()** function. However, sometimes we just want the sprite to disappear when it hits any edge of the screen. The **Sprite.Move()** function will do this for you!

```
Public Sub Move(ByVal screenSize As Point)
```

The input parameter is a **Point** which contains the screen's width and height. When the sprite is moved with the **Move()** function, when it touches any edge of the screen the **IsAlive** property will automatically be set to **False**. We'll use this **Sprite.Move()** function in the next activity!

Your Turn! The Ice Cream Toss Game

For the rest of this chapter, we will be working with a gravity-dependant game called "Ice Cream Toss". This game involves two main elements: an ice-cream cannon on the left side of the screen and a giant ice cream cone on the right side of the screen. The purpose of the game is to fill the ice cream cone by hitting the ice cream cone three times with ice cream scoops shot out of the cannon. You can adjust the angle of the ice cream cannon with the left and right arrow keys and shoot ice cream from the cannon by pressing the spacebar key. The longer you hold down the spacebar, the faster the ice cream will shoot from the cannon. To keep track of your speed, we have a progress bar at the bottom of the screen. This bar will show how powerful the shot is as you hold down the spacebar key.

Here is what the game will look like:

The starter project for this activity can be found in your "**\KidCoder\Game Programming\Activity Starters\Ice Cream Toss**" directory. The name of the solution for this chapter is "**Ice Cream Toss.sln**". Go ahead and open up the Visual Basic 2010 Express software and load this solution.

The starter project has completed most of the basic program code for you. The graphics, key handling, timer methods, and paint functions are already done. Here is a summary of the functions in the game that are completed for you in the activity starter:

IceCreamForm_Load	Calls **StartGame** ()
StartGame	Initializes all the sprites and starts the timer
IceCreamForm_KeyDown	Processes the left and right arrow keys and the space bar
IceCreamForm_KeyUp	When the space bar is released, shoots the ice cream from the cannon
TossTimer_Tick	Moves the ice cream, checks for collisions, and calculates the initial velocity
IceCreamForm_Paint	Paints the cannon, ice cream cone, and shots
CalculateWind	Calculates a random wind speed (used in the next lesson!)

In this activity you will add the ability to shoot the ice cream scoops at the cone. You will need to complete the functions **ShootIceCream**(), **MoveIceCream**() and **CheckCollisions**() functions.

ShootIceCream	Starts the ice cream at the mouth of the cannon with the initial velocity
MoveIceCream	Applies gravity and moves the ice cream shot
CheckCollisions	Determines if the ice cream shot has hit the cone

The following variables are pre-declared for you at the top of the form and initialized in other methods. You will use them to complete this activity:

`Dim scoopShot As Sprite`	The **Sprite** representing the ice cream shot that will move across the screen
`Dim cannonBarrel As Sprite`	The **Sprite** representing the cannon barrel that will rotate to some angle
`Dim iceCreamConeTop As Sprite`	The **Sprite** representing the top of the ice cream cone (the target for the **scoopShots**)
`Dim iceCreamCone As Sprite`	The **Sprite** representing the ice cream cone bottom
`Dim shootingPoint As Point`	Represents the location of the cannon's mouth where the ice cream appears
`Dim velocity As Double`	The shot power (initial speed) determined by the space bar
`Dim iNumHits As Integer`	The number of times the ice cream cone has been hit

ShootIceCream()

The **ShootIceCream**() method is called when the space bar is released. Within this method you will need to initialize the values for the ice cream **scoopShot** sprite.

When the shot is fired you will want to get the **cannonBarrel**'s current angle in order to initialize the **scoopShot** direction. You will also want to set **scoopShot** position equal to the **shootingPoint** position and call **SetVelocity**() using the **velocity** variable.

Find the empty **ShootIceCream()** method and implement the following logic:

```
Private Sub ShootIceCream()
End Sub
```

- Check the **scoopShot.IsAlive** value. If this value is **True**, then there is still a shot in the air. Since we only allow one shot at a time in this game, you will do nothing in this case.
- If the **scoopShot.IsAlive** value is **False**, you can go ahead and initialize the ice cream scoop by setting the following **scoopShot** properties:
  - Set the **scoopShot.IsAlive** value to **True**.
  - Set the **scoopShot.TimeToLive** to 400.
  - Set the angle of the ice cream shot (**scoopShot.Angle**) equal to the cannon barrel's angle.
  - Set the **MaxSpeed** of the scoop to 10 (so our shot doesn't break the sound barrier!)
  - Call **SetVelocity()** on the ice cream shot using the **velocity** variable.
  - Set the **UpperLeft** location of the **scoopShot** equal to the **shootingPoint**.

Now that you have completed the function to initialize the ice cream shot, it's time to make it move across the screen!

MoveIceCream()

Find the empty **MoveIceCream()** method and implement the following logic:

```
Private Sub MoveIceCream()
End Sub
```

- Check to see if the **scoopShot** is alive.
- If the shot is alive, then:
  - Call the **scoopShot.Accelerate()** function with a 0 value for the X acceleration and a 0.04 value for the Y acceleration. This will cause the scoop to fall in an arc, just like any object that is tossed into the air.
  - Call the **scoopShot.Move()** function, and pass in the **Me.ClientSize** value so the function knows how far the sprite can move across the screen. If the sprite reaches the edge of the screen it will become "dead" and the player can shoot again.

CheckCollisions()

Next we need to figure out if your ice cream shot has hit the target! Find the empty **CheckCollisions()** method and implement the following logic:

```
Private Sub CheckCollisions()
End Sub
```

- Check to see if the **scoopShot** is alive.
- If it is, then:
  - See if the **scoopShot** sprite has hit the **iceCreamConeTop** sprite by calling the **IsCollided()** function.

```
If scoopShot.IsCollided(iceCreamConeTop) Then
```

- If it has collided, then:
  - Set the **scoopShot.isAlive** property to **False**
  - Increase the count of **iNumHits** by one
  - Check the value of **iNumHits**
  - If the user has hit the cone three times
    - Stop the **TossTimer**
    - Invalidate the screen so it will repaint
    - Pop-up a message box that tells the user they have won the game.

 Now when you build and run the program you should be able to shoot the ice cream across the screen in a realistic, gravity-controlled parabolic arc. If the ice cream misses then you'll get another shot. If it hits then the cone will fill up a little bit. After three hits you've won the game!

Lesson Three: Wind Acceleration

Up until now, we have only thought about objects flying through the air without any wind to blow them around. In this lesson, we will take a look at what happens to objects that are flying through windy conditions and discuss how to simulate the wind in our Ice Cream Toss game.

Wind affects almost every projectile in the air. Golfers often check the wind before lining up their shots. Paper airplanes fly further if they are propelled by the wind, and baseball players may hit more home runs with the wind at their back than with the wind blowing in their face. If your game involves flying objects you may want to add the effects of wind to increase the realism of your game.

So how do we add wind to a game? In the last lesson, we learned that gravity is a constant acceleration in the Y direction but did not affect the X velocity. The force of gravity caused our projectile to move in an arc on the screen. Wind, on the other hand, can be considered a constant acceleration in the X direction. A wind blowing in the left direction would be a negative X acceleration, and wind blowing in the right direction would be a positive X acceleration.

The wind can have a powerful affect on the velocity and path of a projectile. Consider the following illustration of a paper airplane in flight:

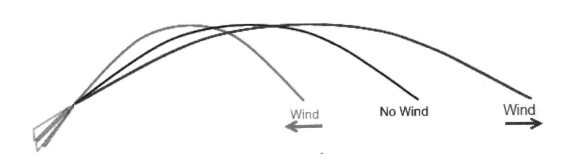

The paper airplane is thrown three different times from the same initial starting location, direction, and speed. The middle line represents the path that the airplane will take if there is no wind at all. With no wind, only the force of gravity affects the plane's path.

The longer gray line shows the path the airplane will take if the wind is heading in the same direction as the airplane. This type of wind is called a "tailwind", which is any wind that is travelling in the same direction as the projectile. The airplane will travel much further with a tailwind!

The shorter gray line shows the path the airplane will take when the wind is travelling in the opposite direction of the airplane. This type of wind is called a "headwind". With a headwind, the airplane's flight will be much shorter!

How do you create the effects of wind in your game? Easy! You already have an acceleration function that will split apart acceleration in either the X or Y direction. You added gravity to the shot by using acceleration in the Y direction in the previous lesson. The wind can just be thought of as acceleration in the X direction. A positive X acceleration will simulate a wind that travels from left to right on the screen. A negative X acceleration will simulate a wind that travels from right to left on the screen.

Since our ice cream shot is moving from left to right, a positive X acceleration will be a tailwind. In order to apply both gravity and a tailwind to the plane at the same time you can make one function call like this:

```
paperAirplane.Accelerate(0.03, 0.04)
```

If we wanted to apply both a headwind and gravity to our airplane, we would use a negative X acceleration instead:

```
paperAirplane.Accelerate(-0.03, 0.04)
```

Just like the value for gravity, you may have to "play" with the size of the X acceleration values to get something that feels realistic in your game environment.

Your Turn! Huff and Puff

In this activity you will add the effects of wind to your Ice Cream Toss game. Your wind will blow either in the left or right direction on the screen. The path the ice cream shot travels will be shortened or lengthened depending on the direction and strength of the wind. A positive wind acceleration (in the right direction) will propel the shot faster; a negative wind acceleration (in the left direction) will slow down the shot.

The following variable has already been declared at the top of the form:

```
Dim currentWind As Double
```

Your project contains a completed function called **CalculateWind**(). This function will generate a random number between -.03 and +.03 and assign it to **currentWind**. This range gives a good illusion of wind effects on the screen.

To use the wind acceleration in the game, you will need to do the following:

- Find the existing Label control named **WindLabel** on the form design page. Set the **Visible** property to **True** so the user can see it. This label will be used to display the current wind speed and direction to the user.

- Add a call to the **CalculateWind**() function in your **CheckCollisions**() function, just after you increase the value of **iNumHits**. This will set a new value for the wind after each hit.

- In the **MoveIceCream**() function, change the call to the **scoopShot.Accelerate**() function to use the **currentWind** value for the X component:

```
scoopShot.Accelerate(currentWind, 0.04)
```

Now when you build and run your game you should see a wind speed indicator at the top that ranges from +100% (strong left-to-right tailwind) to -100% (strong right-to-left headwind). The arc of the ice cream shot should be shortened or lengthened based on the wind speed and direction.

Chapter Review

- Game physics makes a game more realistic by making the objects appear to obey the laws of physics.

- Some common elements of game physics are reflection, gravity, and wind effects.

- Reflection is what happens to an object when it hits a flat surface.

- The Law of Reflection states that when an object hits a flat surface at an angle, it will reflect (bounce) back at the same angle to the perpendicular.

- For a moving **Sprite**, reflection off of a vertical line or the left/right sides of the screen can be achieved by reversing (changing the sign of) the X velocity of the object.

- For a moving **Sprite**, reflection off of a horizontal line or the top/bottom sides of the screen can be achieved by reversing (changing the sign of) the Y velocity of the object.

- In the real world, gravity is a constant force which pulls all objects toward the center of the Earth.

- When an object is thrown in the air, it follows an arc-shaped path back down to the ground.

- To add "gravity" to a game, we can apply a constant acceleration in the Y "down" direction during each timer tick.

- Wind can be represented as a constant acceleration in the X direction (left or right)

- To add "wind" to a game, apply a constant acceleration in the X direction during each timer tick.

All of the Your Turn activities for this chapter have already been completed during the chapter lessons!

Chapter Thirteen: Drawing Text and Printing

In this chapter you will learn some new ways to draw text on the screen in different shapes and sizes. You will also learn how to print the form's screen contents to your printer!

Lesson One: Printing Text on the Screen

So far we have always printed text on the screen in a label or a text box control. In this lesson, we will learn how to write text directly on the screen using some graphics functions.

The label and text box controls are simple and easy-to-use controls. They are great for programs that want to present a standard-looking screen with familiar Windows buttons. But what if we aren't sure where the text will appear beforehand? Or what if we need to move the text during the course of the game? Even better, what if we want to write our text vertically or add some special effects? The label and text box controls cannot do these things.

A more powerful way to display text on the screen is to draw it ourselves from within the form's **Paint** function. The **Graphics** object has a function called **DrawString()** that will do exactly that! **DrawString()** has several different forms depending on your needs. We will describe two of the forms here and you can review others in the MSDN documentation.

```
Public Sub DrawString (s As String, font As Font, brush As Brush, _
                       point As PointF)

Public Sub DrawString (s As String, font As Font, brush As Brush, _
                       point As PointF, format As StringFormat )
```

The function has four or five parameters depending on which form you use.

s	This **String** contains the text that you will be drawing on the screen.
font	The **Font** sets the size and style of the individual letters (see below).
brush	The **Brush** will be used to paint the string on the screen. This is usually a **SolidBrush**, but you can use any **Brush** type like **HatchBrush** or **GradientBrush.**
point	The **Point** sets the upper-left coordinate at which to start drawing the text.
format	The **StringFormat** determines any other special effects to be used (see below).

You already have a good understanding of the **String**, **Brush**, and **Point** data types from earlier chapters. The **Font** and **StringFormat** data types, however, are new to you.

Fonts

A font is a complete set of characters (letters, numbers and symbols) that are created in a specific, artistic style. If you have ever used a word-processing program you may be familiar with the concept of fonts. Different fonts have individual styles and characteristics. There are many different fonts in existence today! Here are some sample fonts:

This is the Arial font.

This is the Licida Calligraphy script font.

THIS IS A STENCIL FONT.

This is the Courier New Font.

Fixed and Variable Width Fonts

Originally, all fonts were created with a fixed width for each character. This made it very easy for the early computers to print text on the screen. Each letter took up the exact same number of pixels in width. Later, variable-width fonts were created. Variable-width fonts gave slim characters like the letters "l", "i", and "t" a smaller width than the widest characters like "w" and "m". This allowed a computer to display more text in a smaller space. For example, compare the fixed and variable-width fonts below:

This is a line of text.

This is a line of text.

Notice how the second line of text is much slimmer than the first line, even though they show the exact same words. The first line is written with the Courier New font, which is a fixed-width font. The second line is written with the Arial font, which is a variable-width font.

So why do we keep the old, fixed-width fonts around? Sometimes spacing is important; you may want to line up characters in columns for cosmetic or other reasons. It is very hard to line up columns that include variable-width text. Since each letter can be a different width, characters in the same column on different lines can't be visually grouped together. A fixed-width font makes this task very easy, since each letter is the same width. For example, consider the following variable-width and fixed-width examples:

a b c d	a b c d
i j k l	i j k l

Notice how the variable-width letters do not form neat columns, while the fixed-width letters are all directly underneath one another -- yet both groups contain the same letters.

Font Sizes

All fonts use a "font size" to guide how large its letters and symbols appear. Here is an example of different font sizes for the Arial font:

This is a size 10 font.

This is a size 16 font.

This is a size 28 font.

Most fonts will be displayed in sizes 10 - 12 for normal reading, while titles, chapter headings, and other noteworthy sections will be larger.

Using Fonts

In Visual Basic the **Font** data type allows you to set the font type, size, and style to use when drawing text. You declare a variable of type **Font** and initialize it with the **New** keyword. There are several ways to create a **Font** object, but we will focus on the one that takes the following four parameters:

```
Dim myFont As Font = New Font(familyName As String, size As Single, _
                             style As FontStyle, unit As GraphicsUnit)
```

Here is what each **Font** parameter means:

familyName	This **Sstring** is the name of the font that you want to use. Common examples include "Arial", "Verdana", or "Times New Roman".
Size	This number represents the size of the font to be drawn.
Style	The **FontStyle** controls any additional features that you want for your font. You can set one or more of the following styles: FontStyle.**Regular** FontStyle.**Bold**

	FontStyle.**Italic**
	FontStyle.**Underline**
	FontStyle.**Strikeout**
	To use more than one style at a time, combine them with the **Or** operator (**"FontStyle.Bold Or FontStyle.Italic"**)
unit	Always use **GraphicsUnit.Pixel** to show the size parameter is measured in pixels.

Now let's look at an example **Font** declaration and initialization. The following line of code will create "Veranda" font that is 12 pixels high and bold-faced:

```
Dim myFont As Font = New Font("Verdana", 12, FontStyle.Bold, _
                        GraphicsUnit.Pixel)
```

You can then use the **myFont** variable anywhere a **Font** is needed like in **Graphics.DrawString()**.

StringFormat

The **DrawString()** function also takes a parameter called **StringFormat**. A **StringFormat** data type is used to set certain directional flags for the text output. This is an optional parameter for **DrawString()**; if you just want to add a normal string of text, you do not need to include a **StringFormat**.

The **StringFormat** data type has several properties, but we'll only describe the most useful one here.

StringFormat.FormatFlags	**FormatFlags** is an enumeration of the following values: **StringFormatFlags.DirectionRightToLeft** **StringFormatFlags.DirectionVertical**

Use **StringFormatFlags.DirectionRightToLeft** when you want to write the string backwards on the screen. Use **StringFormatFlags.DirectionVertical** to draw the text vertically on the screen.

Here is an example of how to create **FormatFlags** of each type:

```
Dim backwardsFormat As StringFormat = New StringFormat
backwardsFormat.FormatFlags = StringFormatFlags.DirectionRightToLeft

Dim verticalFormat As StringFormat = New StringFormat
verticalFormat.FormatFlags = StringFormatFlags.DirectionVertical
```

Now you can use the **backwardsFormat** or **verticalFormat** in the **DrawString()** method when you want to use those special effects.

For example, this call to **DrawString()** will print some text vertically on the screen:

```
Dim myFont As Font = New Font("Verdana", 16, FontStyle.Bold, _
                        GraphicsUnit.Pixel)

Dim redBrush As New SolidBrush(Color.Red)
Dim verticalFormat As StringFormat = New StringFormat
verticalFormat.FormatFlags = StringFormatFlags.DirectionVertical

myGraphics.DrawString("I'm falling", myFont, redBrush, 30, 20,
```

The resulting text would look like this:

Creating Shadow Effects

You can also create your own text effects with a little creativity. To make your text look like it has a 3D shadow, you can just call the **DrawString()** function twice. The first call will use the desired text, size, font, and black brush. The second call will use the same text, size, and font but use a colored brush and offset the starting location by a couple of pixels in each direction. Make sure to draw the shadow (black) version first and then the colored version on top of it! For example:

```
myGraphics.DrawString("Shadow", myFont, blackBrush, 102, 202)
myGraphics.DrawString("Shadow", myFont, redBrush,   100, 200)
```

Here is the resulting output: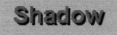

Now that you understand a number of ways to use **DrawString()**, let's put this function to work in an activity!

Your Turn! Word Search

In this activity, we will create a new game called **Word Search**. This game will ask a user for some words. The game will then place those words on a character grid starting at a random location and running in a random direction (including diagonal and backwards!). The words will then be "hidden" by surrounding them with random letters in the rest of the grid. The object of the game is to find all of the hidden words on the page.

This game will simply draw the letters on the screen and then give the user the opportunity to print out the page so they can complete the game. This activity will focus on drawing the letters using **DrawString()**. The next lesson and activity will show how to print the form's screen to the printer!

The starter project for this activity can be found in your "**\KidCoder\Game Programming\Activity Starters\Word Search**" directory. The name of the solution for this chapter is "**Word Search.sln**". Go ahead and open up the Visual Basic 2010 Express software and load this solution.

The starter project has pre-written most of the game logic for you. You will focus on drawing the characters using **DrawString()** in the **Paint()** function.

Paint() Function

You will implement the form's **Paint()** function in order to display the character grid. The game has pre-defined some variables at the top of the form that you will use in order to figure out what and where to draw!

`Const NUM_ROWS As Integer`	This constant sets the number of rows in the grid
`Const NUM_COLUMNS As Integer`	This contant sets the number of columns in the grid
`Const NUM_HIDDEN_WORDS As Integer`	This constant sets how many words will be hidden
`Dim cellSize As Integer`	This variable sets the square cell size in pixels. Use it to help determine your font size.

`Dim characterGrid( _`
`    NUM_COLUMNS - 1, _`
`    NUM_ROWS - 1)  As Char`
	This 2D array holds the individual characters to be drawn in the grid. All of the characters have already been initialized for you, so you just need to draw them!

The initial value of the **NUM_ROWS** and **NUM_COLUMNS** constants is 15 and the initial value of **NUM_HIDDEN_WORDS** is 4. Since we have made these values constants at the top of the program, you can change the size of the grid and the number of hidden words at any time just by changing those values.

Now you will need to write the **Paint()** function that will draw the letters in the grid on the screen. The labels, "Print" button, and other graphical elements are already part of the form and will show automatically.

```
Private Sub WordForm_Paint(ByVal sender As Object, _
                        ByVal e As System.Windows.Forms.PaintEventArgs) _
                        Handles Me.Paint



End Sub
```

You will need to add the following code to **Paint()**:

- Declare and initialize a **Graphics** variable (named **myGraphics**) using the e.Graphics parameter
- Declare and initialize a **SolidBrush** variable (named **WordBrush**) using **Color.Black**
- Declare and initialize a **Font** variable (named **drawFont**) using the following parameters
    - "Courier New" font name
    - **cellSize** - 2 (this font size makes each letter just small enough to fit in a cell)
    - **FontStyle.Regular** - nothing fancy here!
    - **GraphicsUnit.Pixel** - because we calculated font size in pixels
- Create a double loop that will loop through the rows and column in the grid.

```
For i = 0 To NUM_COLUMNS - 1    ' i will be the X-index for the cell
    For j = 0 To NUM_ROWS - 1    ' j will be the Y-index for the cell


    Next
Next
```

- Inside the inner **For** loop we are processing one cell in the grid as determined by the (**i**, **j**) indexes into the 2D array.
  - Calculate the upper-left X and Y coordinate for this cell by using the cell size and the cell's X and Y index:

```
Dim cellX As Integer = i * cellSize
Dim cellY As Integer = j * cellSize
```

  - Use the **DrawString**() function to write the letter contained in this cell to the screen at the **cellX** and **cellY** coordinates you just calculated.
    - Use the brush, font, and upper-left coordinates you created earlier.
    - The letter (string parameter) for each cell is in the **characterGrid** 2D array which can be accessed using your column and row indices again:

```
characterGrid(i, j)
```

 Now when you build and run the program, you will be asked to enter 4 words. Then the program will display a word-search grid containing all of those words in some random location and direction, hidden by a bunch of other random letters.

Remember, if you want to use more or fewer words, you can just change the **NUM_HIDDEN_WORDS** constant at the top of your form!

The "Print" button is not yet functional, but that will change soon!

Lesson Two: Using the Printer

So far we have spent lots of time drawing graphics and text to the computer screen. In this lesson we will show how to print the screen to your printer! The technique is very similar to drawing to the screen -- you are just "drawing" to the printer instead! If you do not have a printer attached to your computer you can still learn the techniques and implement the activity at the end...but you just won't be able to actually test the print function in the **Word Search** game.

PrintDocument Control

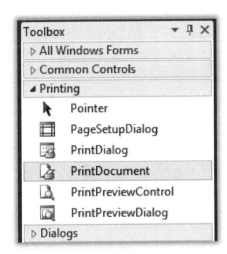

The **PrintDocument** control will be used to enable printing in your program. The control can be found in your Visual Basic Express Toolbox under the heading "Printing". You can drag **PrintDocument** to your form like any other control.

PrintDocument will show up at the bottom of the design screen, similar to a **Timer** control, because the **PrintDocument** control is not visible to the user.

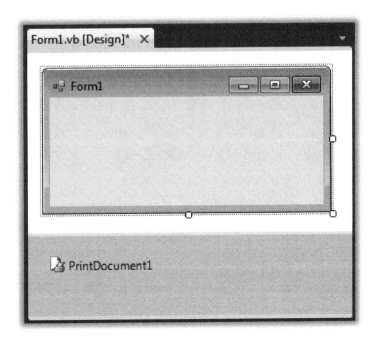

When you want to start printing, call the **Print**() method on the **PrintDocument** control variable:

```
PrintDocument1.Print()
```

Calling the **PrintDocument.Print**() function will cause another event function to be executed -- the **PrintDocument.PrintPage**() event function. You can create this function just by double-clicking on the **PrintDocument1** variable on your form design screen!

The **PrintPage** event works just like the **Paint**() event for a form. However, instead of sending the graphics to the screen, **PrintPage** will be sending the graphics to the printer. The **PrintPage** event function looks like this:

```
Private Sub PrintDocument1_PrintPage(sender As Object, _
              e As System.Drawing.Printing.PrintPageEventArgs)
```

As you can see, this looks almost exactly like the **Paint**() event. **PrintPage**() includes the same "e" parameter that we will use to get a copy of our **Graphics** object (again, just like we do in the **Paint** event).

```
Dim printGraphics As Graphics = e.Graphics
```

Then we can call any of the same graphics functions that we have already learned about earlier in the course. For instance, the following call to **DrawLine**() works exactly as you expect, except the line will be sent to the printer instead of the screen:

```
printGraphics.DrawLine(linePen, startX, startY, endX, endY)
```

So, in order to print your form's contents to the printer, you will need to write some code into the **PrintDocument.PrintPage**() function to recreate the screen's graphics in a manner similar to the **Paint**() method.

PrintDialog

Now we have a control that will handle the printing of our graphics, but how do we start the print job? We could just create a button on our form that, when clicked, calls the **Print**() method of our **PrintDocument** control. However, this would just send our graphics straight to the printer without asking the user which printer to use, how many copies to print, and so on. We want our print job to have the same sort of options you expect to see in other professional word processing or graphics programs. So instead of connecting a button directly to the **PrintDocument** control, we will use another built-in control called **PrintDialog**.

PrintDialog is another common dialog box like the **OpenFileDialog** and the **SaveFileDialog**. The **PrintDialog** control is located in the Toolbox under the heading "Printing". Once this control is added to your form, it will show up at the bottom of the design window just like the **PrintDocument** control.

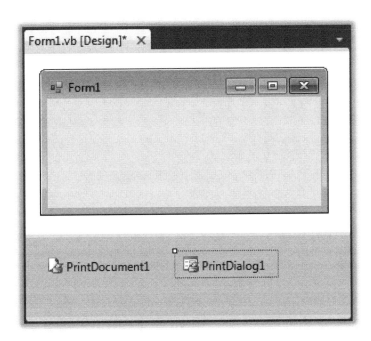

In order to show the print dialog window on the screen, you will need to call the **PrintDialog.ShowDialog()** method, like this:

```
PrintDialog1.ShowDialog()
```

Here is what the **PrintDialog** looks like when it is shown. The exact number and type of printers shown will depend on your own computer setup.

This is much better! Now the user can choose which printer they want to use, how many copies to make and any other printer preferences that are supported by their chosen printer.

If the user clicks "OK" or "Print" to print, you will get a **DialogResult.OK** returned from **ShowDialog()**.

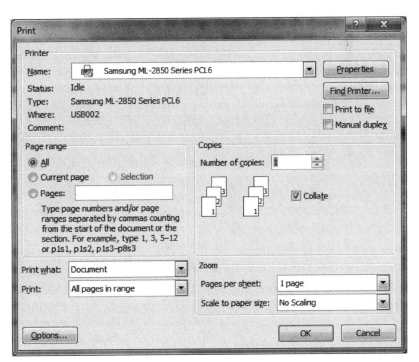

Perhaps the best feature of the **PrintDialog** is that you can easily connect it to an existing **PrintDocument** control. In the properties window for the **PrintDialog**, you will see an item that says "Document". If you click on the property, it will drop down a list of all of the **PrintDocuments** in your project, as seen here:

By choosing our **PrintDocument** control (in this case the "PrintDocument1"), the two printing controls are linked. This means that any setting the user selects in the **PrintDialog** screen will be automatically communicated to the **PrintDocument** when it's time to actually print the page. So we don't have to worry about what printer the user wants to use, or how many copies they want to print. This is all done for us!

The overall sequence of events can be a bit confusing, so let's summarize:

- Link your **PrintDocument** to your **PrintDialog** control in the **PrintDialog** Properties screen
- While running your program, the user clicks the "Print" button
- In the "Print" button event handler function
  - You call **PrintDialog1.ShowDialog()** to show the Print Dialog screen
  - You check the **DialogResult** from **ShowDialog()**. If the user has clicked "OK", then
    - You call the **PrintDocument1.Print()** function
    - Your **PrintDocment1 PrintPage** event handler function will be called
    - Your **PrintPage** function should "draw" the graphics to the printer paper

Formatting a Page for Printing

Since the **Paint** event and the **PrintPage** event are so similar, you could just copy the code from the **Paint** event and paste it into the **PrintPage** event. This would probably work, but it wouldn't be ideal. Why? Because your form is probably only a couple of inches wide and a couple of inches high, whereas your paper is typically 8.5 inches wide and 11 inches tall! If you just print the same size graphics on your paper, it will not take up the entire paper and will end up looking tiny and off-center on the page.

You will usually want to re-format the graphics and text on your screen before you send them out to the printer. The "e" variable in the **PrintPage** event will give us the upper-left corner and size of the printable area of the paper.

e.MarginBounds	This **Rectangle** represents the area within the margins on the page. • The **Left** and **Top** properties show the upper-left coordinate of the printable area. • The **Width** and **Height** properties show the size of the printable area.

Just like the form's width and height are used to determine size and location of objects on the screen, the **MarginBounds** can be used to determine the size and location of objects on the printed page.

In the case of our Word Search program, recall that our normal **Paint**() function started painting at (0,0) and used the **cellSize** variable to set the width and height of each cell. Clearly, when we print to a larger piece of paper, those values will need to change! This is exactly what you are going to do in the next activity.

Your Turn! Print the Word Search

In this activity you will add the ability to print the Word Search game you finished in the last lesson. Go ahead and open the Visual Basic 2010 Express software and continue with the "**Word Search.sln**" solution.

The activity starter project already includes the **PrintDocument** and **PrintDialog** controls placed on the form. Make sure that the **PrintDialog1.Document** property is set to the **PrintDocument1** control. This will ensure that any settings the user picks in the Print Dialog screen will be automatically used by your **PrintDocument1** control.

Now you will need to finish two functions to complete the printing project.

PrintButton_Click()

Complete the **PrintButton_Click()** method so it launches the printing process. To do this, add the following to this function:

```
Private Sub PrintButton_Click(ByVal sender As System.Object, _
                    ByVal e As System.EventArgs) Handles PrintButton.Click

End Sub
```

- Create a variable called **results** with type **DialogResults**
- Call the **ShowDialog()** function on the **PrintDialog1** control. Set the **results** variable equal to the return value of this function.
- Check to see if the value of **results** is equal to **DialogResult.OK**. If it does, call the **PrintDocument1.Print()** function.

Now, when you build and run your program the on-screen graphics shouldn't change at all. But when you click the "Print" button the print dialog popup will display. If you select a printer and click "OK" or "Print", you should get a blank piece of paper from the printer.

Your **PrintPage()** function is not yet completed, so nothing will appear on the paper! Let's fix that right away!

PrintPage()

Next, you will need to finish the code for the **PrintDocument1_PrintPage()** function. The activity starter has already done some of the set-up work in this function with the following code:

```vb
Private Sub PrintDocument1_PrintPage(ByVal sender As Object, _
                    ByVal e As System.Drawing.Printing.PrintPageEventArgs) _
                    Handles PrintDocument1.PrintPage

    'Create a graphics object for our printed page
    Dim printGraphics As Graphics = e.Graphics

    'Create a brush that will be used to paint the letters on the page
    Dim WordBrush As New SolidBrush(Color.Black)

    'Create a pen that will be used to paint the line between
    'the grid and the word key
    Dim linePen As New Pen(Color.Black, 2)

    'letterwidth and letterheight are used to figure out how big to make
    'letters on the paper and to increment the 'lines' that are printed

    Dim letterWidth As Integer = e.MarginBounds.Width / NUM_COLUMNS

    ' Add 3 lines for word key verbage and then lines for hidden words
    Dim letterHeight As Integer = e.MarginBounds.Height / _
                        (NUM_ROWS + 3 + NUM_HIDDEN_WORDS)

    'These variables hold the current x & y positions for letter being drawn
    Dim currentXposition, currentYPosition As Integer
```

The width of each letter width is determined by dividing the width of the printable area of the page by the number of columns that we need to print.

The height calculation is a bit more complicated. We cannot just divide the height of the printable page by the number of rows that we need to print, since we also need to leave room for the Word Key at the bottom of the page. So we divide the height by the total number of lines that we need to print. We reserve a line for each grid row (NUM_ROWS), plus 3 lines for the space between the grid and the word key, plus a line for each hidden word (NUM_HIDDEN_WORDS).

Below all of this starter logic, you will need to add some more code to finish the function!

The first thing you should do is create a **Font** that you will use to draw the text on the page. Name this new font **printFont**. You will want to use a fixed-width font such as "Courier New" to keep the letters nicely aligned on the page. Set the font size to be 2 pixels smaller than the **letterWidth** to leave some room around the letters in the grid. Use **FontStyle.Regular** and **GraphicsUnit.Pixel** for the remaining parameters.

Next, create a double **For** loop that will walk through the rows and columns in the grid. Remember how you did this in the **Paint**() function!

- For each cell in the grid:
  - Calculate the current X and Y positions where you will draw the letter. These calculations should look similar to the logic that we used to determine the cell placement in the **Paint**() function. However, use **letterWidth** and **letterHeight** variables instead of **cellSize**, and also add in the **e.MarginBounds.Left** or **e.MarginBounds.Top** to start the grid at the right spot. For example:

```
currentXposition = e.MarginBounds.Left + (i * letterWidth)
currentYPosition = e.MarginBounds.Top + (j * letterHeight)
```

  - Use the **DrawString**() function to print out each cell's letter, using your **Font**, **WordBrush**, **currentXposition** and **currentYPosition**.

 Now when you build and run your program, and click the "Print" button, you should see the letter grid printed out to your selected printer with nicely spaced and positioned letters. However, we still need to draw the line and show the list of hidden words!

To draw the separator line, after the **For** loops you should:

- Reset the **currentXposition** to the **e.MarginBounds.Left** value.
- Skip two lines on the page by adding two **letterHeight** values to the **currentYPosition**.
- Use the **DrawLine**() function to draw a line on the page from a point at the **currentXposition** and **currentYposition** to a point at the **e.MarginBounds.Right** and **currentYposition**. Use the **linePen** that was already declared for you.

```
printGraphics.DrawLine(linePen, currentXposition, currentYPosition, _
                    e.MarginBounds.Right, currentYPosition)
```

To show the list of hidden words, after drawing the line above you should:

- Skip another line on the page.
- Use the **DrawString**() function to print the Word Key header ("Words to Find:") at the **currentXposition** and **currentYposition**.
- Skip another line on the page by increasing **currentYPosition**.
- Create a **For** loop to walk through the **hiddenWords String** array. For each string in the array:
  - Use the **DrawString**() function to print the string on the page, using your **Font, WordBrush, currentXPosition** and **currentYPosition**.
    - Note: You may want to print the upper case version of the words to match the letters in the grid. (**hiddenWords(i).ToUpper**())
  - Skip a line on the page before looping to the next element in the array

 **You have now finished your printing code. If you run the program and click "Print", select a target printer, and click "OK" on the Print dialog, you should get a full-page version of your form window printed to paper, including grid, separating line, and list of hidden words!**

If you do not have a printer attached to your computer, that's OK! The printer list in the print dialog popup will be empty, and you can just hit "Cancel" to avoid printing anything.

Chapter Review

- Labels and Text Box controls are useful when you want to write normal text without any special effects.

- When you want to draw text with special effects, or you don't know exactly how many text objects will be displayed in advance, you will want to use the **Graphics.DrawString()** method.

- The **DrawString()** method allows you to write text vertically or backwards. You can add **bold**, underline, *italic*, or ~~strikeout~~ effects.

- The **StringFormat** parameter of the **DrawString()** function will allow you to set special text drawing formats, like vertical and backwards text.

- **Fonts** are complete sets of characters that are created with specific styles and sizes.

- The **DrawString()** method allows you to write text in any font, color, and texture that you desire.

- Variable-width fonts are useful for fitting a large amount of text in a small space.

- Fixed-width fonts are useful when you need to line up columns of data.

- You can create a 3D shadow effect by printing a black version of the text underneath the top-level colored text and slightly offsetting the location.

- In order to print a page in Visual Basic, you can use a **PrintDocument** control's **PrintPage()** function.

- **PrintPage()** works just like the **Paint()** function for a form. Instead of painting the screen, however, **PrintPage()** paints graphics and text to a printer.

- The **PrintPage()** function contains a graphics object that you can use to perform all of the graphics tasks that we have demonstrated in this course.

- The **PrintDialog** control is a special dialog that will let users choose printers and options before printing a page.

- When formatting a document for printing, you should remember that a printed page is usually larger than a screen and will probably have a different rectangular shape.

- The **MarginBounds** property found in the **PrintPage()** "e" parameter will help you to figure out how much space you have on the paper when you are printing.

All of the Your Turn activities for this chapter have already been completed during the chapter lessons!

Chapter Fourteen: Final Project

In this chapter you will apply what you have learned in this course to create one final game. We will provide the game description and a programming plan, but you will be responsible for most of the creative effort!

Lesson One: Chain Reaction

The game you will be creating is a simple two-player strategy game called "Chain Reaction" or, more commonly, just "Chain".

The Chain game starts with a board that is a grid of empty cells. The game grid typically has five or more rows and columns. The starting game board is shown to the right.

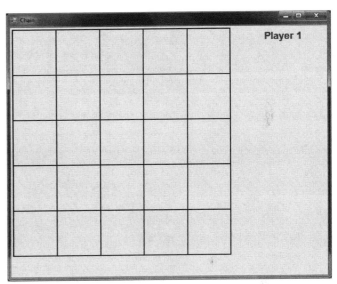

Players will take turns clicking one cell in the grid with the mouse. When a player clicks on the cell, a small dot will appear. Each player's dots will have a different color. The color of the dot will help to show which user "owns" that cell – blue for Player 1 and red for Player 2.

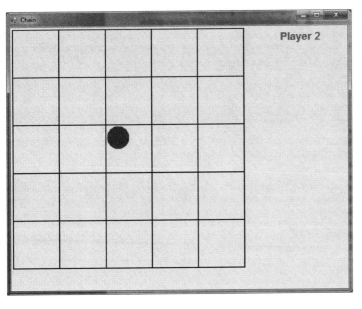

The screen to the left shows one blue dot has been placed in a cell by Player 1.

On each turn, players can choose to add a dot to an empty cell or a cell that the player already "owns" with one or more colored dots. A player cannot click on the other player's cells. If they click on a cell that already has one of their dots on it, another dot will appear. When the cell has 4 dots on it, it will "explode".

The screen shot below shows the game after the players have taken several turns. Notice that the center cell has 3 blue dots in it. If the blue player places one more dot into this cell it will explode!

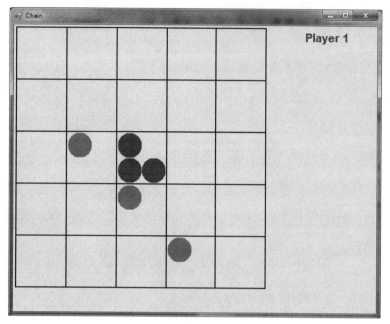

When the dot "explodes", it will send 1 small dot in all directions (up, down, left and right). The original cell (where the explosion originated) will be left empty. If an "exploded" small dot lands on a cell that already has one or more dots in it, it will just add another dot to the cell. If that cell belongs to the other player, it will claim that cell for the current player, changing the color of all dots in the cell. If that cell already has 3 dots in it, the new dot will cause this cell to also "explode". This can set off a series of chain reactions, which is where the game gets its name.

The image to the right shows a continuation of the screen shown above. When the blue player clicks the center cell to add the fourth dot, the cell will explode, throwing 1 small blue dot in each of the 4 possible directions.

You can see that center cell which had the 3 blue dots is now empty. The cells above and to the right of that center cell now have one blue dot. The cells to the left and bottom of the original cell used to have 1 red dot on them. When a blue dot is added to those cells from the center explosion, the red dots are changed to blue and 1 more dot is added (making 2 in each cell).

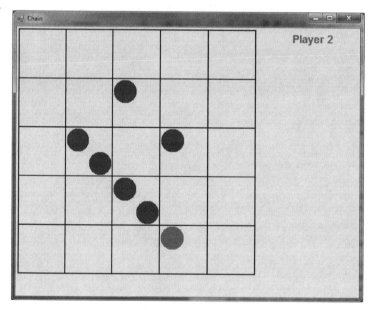

The game will end when one player does not own any squares with dots on the board. When this occurs, we will display a message box that congratulates the winner.

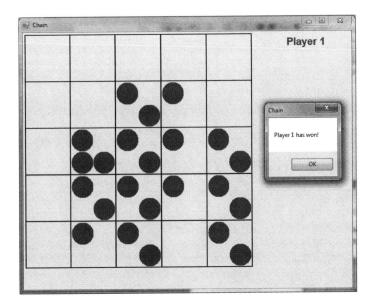

The game of Chain does have some special rules for the side cells and the corner cells. Since the corner cells can only explode in 2 directions, they will explode when they contain 2 dots. Since the edge or side cells can only explode in 3 directions, they will explode when they contain 3 dots.

In the sample below, the players have the maximum amount of dots in all the side and corner squares without causing an explosion. Any play in any of the side or corner squares will result in an explosion! As a matter of fact, Player 2's next move can decide the game! Causing any of the squares to explode will cause a chain reaction that will turn all of the colors red.

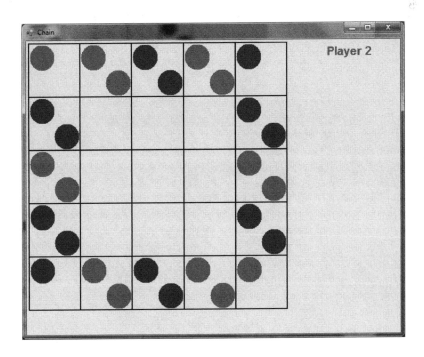

Lesson Two: Creating the Game Board

The activity starter project for the Chain game gives you a few things to help get started. In this lesson we will review the pieces that are already in place in preparation for your first activity!

The starter project contains the following elements:

- The main screen form, named **ChainForm**.

- A label, named **TurnLabel**, which will be used to show which player is the current player.

- Several pre-defined constants that specify different aspects of the game, such as how many rows and columns will appear on the grid.

- An enumeration called **PLAYER**, which has the values **PLAYER.NONE**, **PLAYER.PLAYER1**, and **PLAYER.PLAYER2**.

- The **Sprite** library is included in the project

- The **Cell** data structure has been created for you. This structure includes a **Sprite** variable, an indication of which **PLAYER** owns the cell, and a count of how many dots are in the cell.

- All of the variables in the game state are pre-declared for you. The **GameState** includes a two-dimensional array of **Cells**, and a variable to track the current player.

- A **gameOver** Boolean variable indicates whether or not anyone has won the game

- The **Paint()** event handler function has already been created for you.

- There are several empty functions; these will be your responsibility!

Pre-defined Data structures

Let's take a closer look at some of the structures that have been defined in the activity starter:

A **Cell** data structure will be used to represent one of the cells in the game grid. Each **Cell** will contain a **Sprite**, a variable that will tell which player (if any) owns the cell, and a variable that will track the current number of dots that are in the cell (0, 1, 2, 3, or 4).

```
Private Structure Cell
        Dim mySprite As Sprite
        Dim owningPlayer As Integer
        Dim numDots As Integer
End Structure
```

A **GameState** data structure will be used to hold the game's current state information. This will hold a two-dimensional array of **Cells** and will track which player has the current turn.

```
Private Structure GameState
        Dim cellArray(,) As Cell
        Dim currentPlayer As PLAYER
End Structure
```

The **Player** enumeration contains values that define which player currently owns a cell:

```
Private Enum PLAYER
        NONE = 0
        PLAYER1 = 1
        PLAYER2 = 2
End Enum
```

Finally, a few handy variables have been defined that give us descriptive names and colors for each player.

```
Dim player1Description As String = "Player 1"
Dim player2Description As String = "Player 2"
Dim player1Color As Color = Color.Blue
Dim player2Color As Color = Color.Red
```

Getting Started

The Chain game program will follow a similar pattern to our previous games, where the **Form_Load()** method calls a function called **StartGame()**. The **StartGame()** function will initialize the game state.

The **StartGame()** function for Chain will have a number of responsibilities to initialize the game state. Part of those responsibilities includes initializing the **Cells** in the grid. We have defined an **InitializeGameGrid()** function specifically for this task that you can implement and call from **StartGame()**.

When all game information has been initialized in **StartGame()** the last step will be to call **Invalidate()** in order to repaint the screen. The Form's **Paint()** function has been finished for you to help get started.

The pre-defined **Paint()** function will loop through the cell array and perform the following tasks:
- Define a **Pen** to draw the grid
- Define **Brushes** for each player's color
- Draw a bounding rectangle for each cell. This will give the screen an outlined grid pattern.
- For each cell, if one or more dots are present, draw them in the cell in the owning player's color.

Your Turn! Starting the Game

The starter project for this activity can be found in your "**KidCoder\Game Programming\Activity Starters\Chain**" directory. The name of the solution for this chapter is "**Chain.sln**". Go ahead and start up the Visual Basic 2010 Express software and load the solution. You will build on this solution throughout the rest of the lessons in this chapter.

In this activity, you will complete the code for the **StartGame()** and **InitializeGameGrid()** functions.

StartGame()

A beginning **StartGame()** function has already been defined for you. Find this function in your program.

```
Private Sub StartGame()
```

The first initialization task, resizing the array of **Cells**, has already been done for you.

```
ReDim myGameState.cellArray(NUM_COLUMNS - 1, NUM_ROWS - 1)
```

The two-dimensional **cellArray** will form the grid of cells for the game board.

Now you will need to initialize the rest of the form and game state data as follows:

- Set the **gameOver** Boolean to **False** to show we are starting a new game
- Set the **myGameState.currentPlayer** equal to **PLAYER.PLAYER1**
- Set the **TurnLabel.Text** property to **player1Description**.
- Set the **TurnLabel.ForeColor** property to **player1Color**.
- Determine the size of each cell by measuring the form's dimensions.
  - **If** the form's height (**me.ClientSize.Height**) is greater than its width **me.ClientSize.Width**
    - Set the value of **cellSize** to the form's width divided by the NUM_ROWS
    - Subtract 10 from **cellSize** to give us some extra room around the edges
  - **Else**
    - Set the value of **cellSize** to the form's height divided by the NUM_ROWS
    - Subtract 10 from **cellSize** to give us some extra room around the edges
- Call the **InitializeGameGrid()** function to create the game board grid.
- Call the **Invalidate()** function to refresh the screen.

InitializeGameGrid()

The **InitializeGameGrid**() function has also been started for you. Go ahead and find this function.

```
Private Sub InitializeGameGrid()
```

Inside this function you need to initialize each cell in the game state's **cellArray**. This is conveniently done with an outer **For** loop that walks through each column and an inner **For** loop that walks through each row.

```
For i = 0 To NUM_COLUMNS - 1
    For j = 0 To NUM_ROWS - 1
        'Here you can access the individual cell with cellArray(i, j)
    Next
Next
```

For each cell within the inner **For** loop, you will need to fully initialize each cell in the array. Each cell can be accessed with the phrase "**myGameState.cellArray(i, j)**".

- Set the cell's **owningPlayer** to **PLAYER.NONE**
- Set the cell's **numDots** to 0.
- Set the cell's **mySprite** equal to **New Sprite**
- Set the **Size.X** and **Size.Y** for **mySprite** to the **cellSize** value that was calculated earlier.
- Set the **UpperLeft.X** for **mySprite** to "(i * cellSize + 5)"
- Set the **UpperLeft.Y** for **mySprite** to "(j * cellSize + 5)"
- Set the **mySprite.IsAlive** value to **True**

 At this point, you should be able to start the game and see the game board appear on the screen! There are no dots visible yet though!

Lesson Three: Putting Your Mark on the Board

The two players in this game will use the mouse to interact with the game board. To set a dot on the grid, players will click the left mouse button when the mouse pointer is on the target cell. If the selected cell is empty or already belongs to the current player, a dot will be added to the cell. If the selected cell belongs to the other player a message should pop-up to tell the user that they cannot place their dot in that cell.

Recall that each cell on the board is represented by a **Sprite**. Given the coordinates of a mouse click from the mouse event handler function we can use the **Sprite.IsClicked()** function. This method will return **True** if the mouse click coordinates are within that **Sprite** image on the screen.

```
Public Function IsClicked(ByVal clickPoint As Point)
```

If the player has clicked on a valid cell (the cell is empty or already belongs to this player) the following steps should be taken:

- Increase the number of dots in the selected **Cell** by 1
- Change the selected **Cell's** owner to the current player
- Call a function named **HandleExplosions()** to perform all of the explosive activity that may result
- Check to see if the game is over as a result of all the explosions. If so, call **StartGame()** to launch a new game!
- Update the current player to the next person and change the **TurnLabel**'s text and color accordingly.
- **Invalidate()** the screen to ensure all changes are shown

Your Turn! Making Your Mark

In this activity, you will complete the code for the **MouseClick()** and the **HandleExplosions()** functions.

ChainForm_MouseClick()

Find the empty **ChainForm_MouseClick()** event handler function in the Chain project. In this method you will use the **e.Location** parameter that contains the mouse click coordinates. You will want to compare these coordinates to each **Cell** in the grid to see if the mouse click matches that **Cell**.

In order to compare the mouse click to each **Cell** you will need to loop over the **cellArray** with a double **For** loop again, just like you did in **InitailizeGameGrid()**.

For each **Cell** in the grid, call the **mySprite.IsClicked()** method with **e.Location** as the parameter. When one of the **Cells** returns **True** you have found the target cell for the mouse click! Hint: The current cell can be accessed as **myGameState.cellArray(i, j)**, assuming the **For** loop index variables are **i** for column and **j** for row.

If the target cell has been clicked, do the following:

- Check to see if the cell's **owningPlayer** value equals the **currentPlayer** OR the Cell's **owningPlayer** value equals **PLAYER.NONE**. If so then this is a valid target cell for the player!
    - Add 1 to the **numDots** for this cell and set the cell's **owningPlayer** to the current player (in case it was **PLAYER.NONE**).
    - Call **HandleExplosions()**
    - Check to see if **gameOver** is now **True**. If so,
        - Call **StartGame()** to set up a new game
        - **Return** immediately instead of finishing the rest of the function
    - **If the currentPlayer is PLAYER.PLAYER1** then
        - Change the **currentPlayer** to **PLAYER.PLAYER2**.
        - Set the **TurnLabel.Text** property to **player2Description** and the **TurnLabel.ForeColor** property to **player2Color**.
    - **Else**
        - Change the **currentPlayer** to **PLAYER.PLAYER1**.
        - Set the **TurnLabel.Text** property to **player1Description** and the **TurnLabel.ForeColor** property to **player1Color**.
    - Call **Invalidate()** to refresh the screen.

- Else if the chosen cell is not valid for this player, so display a **MsgBox** telling them to select a another cell.

 Now when you build and run the program, you should be able to see each player put a colored dot in a square according to the rules of the game. However, there are no explosions yet! That is your next job!

HandleExplosions()

The **HandleExplosions()** function has also been started for you. The activity starter contains some skeleton code already to help define the overall flow control. The general idea is that the function must loop until all explosions have completed! Each explosion may in turn cause other explosions. The starter function contains a **Do / Loop While** block that will loop while an **isExploded** Boolean variable stays **True**.

```
Private Sub HandleExplosions()
    Dim isExploded As Boolean

    Do
    isExploded = False

    ' add your code here to complete the function logic

    Loop While isExploded = True
End Sub
```

Within the **Do** loop it's your job to determine if any cell in the grid has enough dots to explode, handle the explosion, and pause for a brief time between explosions so the players can see what's going on.

- Create a double **For** loop that will walk through the 2D **cellArray** (you are an expert by now!)
- Inside the innermost **For** loop:
  - Call the **CheckExplosion(i,j)** function, passing in the **i** and **j** looping index values. In the next lesson you will complete this function which does all the hard work for making an explosion happen.
  - If the **CheckExplosion()** function returns **True**:
    - Set the value of **isExploded** to **True**
    - Add the following line to make the program pause for a half-second:

```
Sleep(500)
```

The **Sleep()** function just makes the computer pause. (The parameter "500" is 500 milliseconds, or ½ a second.) Note that in order to use the **Sleep()** function, you must have this line at the top of your form:

```
Imports System.Threading.Thread
```

We have added this **Imports** statement already in the activity starter.

- Finally, after the call to **Sleep()**, you should check the **gameOver** variable. If **True**, then you don't need to process any more explosions so just **Return** from the function immediately.

 At this point you should be able to start the game and have the players take turns adding dots to the cells in the grid. Though we have some of the code in place to handle explosions, we aren't quite finished yet, so you won't see any difference from the last checkpoint.

In the next lesson you will add the code to actually handle the explosions!

Lesson Four: Blowing Things Up

In this lesson, we will discuss the code necessary to complete the cell explosions. In the last lesson, you created a function called **HandleExplosions**() that made a call to a function called **CheckExplosion**(). Now we must finish the **CheckExplosion()** function.

CheckExplosion() should check a specific cell in the grid to see if it needs to explode. The cell's coordinates will be passed into the function as a column number and row number. The cell is first checked to see where it is in the grid: If it is a corner cell, it will only need 2 dots in it to explode. If it is an edge cell (on the top row, bottom row, first column or last column), it will only need 3 dots in it to explode. All other cells will need to have 4 dots to explode.

Once the function determines how many dots are required to explode this cell, the cell's **numDots** value is checked. If this value is equal to or greater than the number of dots needed to explode, then call an **Explode**() function to take care of all the explosion details. If the **numDots** value is less than the number needed to explode, **CheckExplosion**() will just return a value of **False**.

The **Explode**() function will be responsible for exploding the original cell into the adjacent cells. The original cell's number of dots will be decreased as the adjacent cell's number of dots is increased. For instance, if the original cell needs to explode upward, the original cell's **numDots** is decreased by 1, while the cell directly above is increased by one. This continues for each direction that the cell needs to explode.

If any of the new cells (the cells that have been exploded into) do not belong to the current player, the ownership of that cell is changed. Any cell that the original cell explodes into will now belong to the current player.

After all of original cell's dots have been exploded out into the adjacent cells, check the original cell's **numDots** value. If all of the dots are gone then the cell's **owningPlayer** value should be reset to **PLAYER.NONE**.

Your Turn! Exploding Cells

In this activity, you will complete the code for the **CheckExplosion**() and the **Explode**() functions.

CheckExplosion()

A beginning **CheckExplosion**() function has been defined for you in the activity starter.

```
Private Function CheckExplosion(ByVal ColNum As Integer, _
                                ByVal RowNum As Integer) As Boolean
```

This function takes in two parameters: the column number and row number of the cell that needs to be checked for explosions. These values are passed into this function from the **HandleExplosions**() function you completed in the last activity.

The following variables are already created for you in the function:

```
Dim dotsToExplode As Integer = 4
Dim Up, Down, Left, Right As Boolean
```

The first variable, **dotsToExplode** will be used to decide whether or not the cell is ready to explode. We will start with the assumption that the cell will require 4 dots to explode.

The second list of variables represents the four directions that the dots can possibly explode. You will set these values to either **True** or **False**, depending on where the cell is located in the grid.

In order to complete the function you will need to implement the following logic:

- First, set the values for **Up**, **Down**, **Left**, and **Right** to **True**. This assumes that the cell is not on any edge and will explode dots in all 4 directions.

Next, complete a series of checks to see where the cell is located in the game grid:

- Check to see if the cell is located on the left-most column of the grid. (If the **ColNum** is 0, the cell is in the left column.)
    - Since we will not need to explode in the left direction, set the value of **Left** to **False**.
    - Subtract 1 from the value of **dotsToExplode**.

- Check to see if the cell is located on the top-most row of the grid. (If the **RowNum** is 0, the cell is in the top column.)
  - o Since we will not need to explode in the up direction, set the value of **Up** to **False**.
  - o Subtract 1 from the value of **dotsToExplode**.

- Check to see if the cell is on the bottom row of the grid. (If the **RowNum** is equal to NUM_ROWS – 1, it is on the bottom row.)
  - o Since we will not need to explode downwards, set the value of **Down** to **False**.
  - o Subtract 1 from the value of **dotsToExplode**.

- Check to see if the cell is on the right-most column of the grid. (If the **ColNum** is equal to NUM_COLS – 1, it is in the right column.)
  - o Since we will not need to explode to the right, set the value of **Right** to **False**.
  - o Subtract 1 from the value of **dotsToExplode**.

At this point, the value of **dotsToExplode** should be correct for the cell that is being tested and the values of **Up**, **Down**, **Left** and **Right** are able to tell which direction we need to explode.

For example, consider the scenario where the target cell at (0, 1) is a side cell along the left edge. The **Up**, **Right**, and **Down** variables should all be **True** showing explosions in those directions, while the **Left** variable should be **False**. The **dotsToExplode** should be 3 as that is how many directions the explosion will cover.

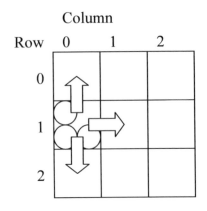

Now you can complete this function!
- If **myGameState.cellArray(ColNum, RowNum).numDots** is greater than or equal to **dotsToExplode**, do the following:
  - o Call the **Explode()** function, passing in **ColNum**, **RowNum**, **Up**, **Down**, **Left**, and **Right**.
  - o Force a repaint of the screen right away (without having to leave the function!):

```
Me.Refresh()
```

  - o **Return True** to the calling function
- Else the **numDots** is not greater than the value of **dotsToExplode**, so all you have to do is:
  - o **Return False** to the calling function

You will notice that we used the function **Me.Refresh()** instead of **Invalidate()** to repaint the game screen. It is very important that this game be able to refresh the screen in between each call to **Explode()**. This way, the players can watch as the chain reactions explode slowly over the screen. The **Invalidate()** function is a very useful, but also a very polite function. It will always wait until the current event handler function has finished executing before it will actually paint the screen. The **Me.Refresh()** command is not at all polite. When you use this command, it will immediately refresh the screen, no matter what the program is currently doing. It does not wait its turn at all! Most of the time, you will want to be polite in your games (and in all things!), but in this case, we need to be a little more demanding!

Explode()

Next, you will need to complete the **Explode()** function. This function will explode the specified cell in the directions that have been determined by the **CheckExplosion()** function.

```
Private Sub Explode(ByVal ColNum As Integer, ByVal RowNum As Integer, _
                    ByVal Up As Boolean, ByVal Down As Boolean, _
                    ByVal Left As Boolean, ByVal Right As Boolean)
```

The function takes six input parameters:

`ColNum`	An integer value that represents the exploding cell's column number
`RowNum`	An integer value that represents the exploding cell's row number
`Up`	A Boolean value that will tell us whether or not to explode in the upward direction
`Down`	A Boolean value that will tell us whether or not to explode in the downward direction
`Left`	A Boolean value that will tell us whether or not to explode in the leftward direction
`Right`	A Boolean value that will tell us whether or not to explode in the rightward direction

There are a lot of parameters to this function, but they will make it very easy for you to distribute the newly exploded dots on the grid. Using the starting **ColNum** and **RowNum** you will check each directional Boolean and, if **True**, add a dot to the cell directly above, below, left, or right of the exploding cell.

Hint: You can access the original cell with the expression

```
myGameState.cellArray(ColNum, RowNum).
```

You can reach the neighboring cells by adding or subtracting 1 from the starting **ColNum** and **RowNum** depending on the direction you are trying to go! This example accesses the cell to the right of the input cell:

```
myGameState.cellArray(ColNum + 1, RowNum)
```

Here what you need to do to complete this function:

- If the value of **Up** is **True**
  - Subtract 1 from the value of the exploding cell's **numDots**
  - Find the cell **above** (**RowNum** - 1) and:
    - Add 1 to its **numDots**
    - Change the value of the cell's **owningPlayer** to the **currentPlayer**
  - Hint: The cell above is **myGameState.cellArray**(ColNum, RowNum − 1)
- If the value of **Down** is **True**
  - Subtract 1 from the value of the exploding cell's **numDots**
  - Find the cell **below** (**RowNum** + 1) and:
    - Add 1 to its **numDots**
    - Change the value of the cell's **owningPlayer** to the **currentPlayer**
  - Hint: The cell below is **myGameState.cellArray**(ColNum, RowNum + 1)
- If the value of **Left** is **True**
  - Subtract 1 from the value of the exploding cell's **numDots**
  - Find the cell **to the left** (**ColNum** − 1) and:
    - Add 1 to its **numDots**
    - Change the value of the cell's **owningPlayer** to the **currentPlayer**
  - Hint: The cell to the left is **myGameState.cellArray**(ColNum − 1, RowNum)
- If the value of **Right** is **True**
  - Subtract 1 from the value of the exploding cell's **numDots**
  - Find the cell **to the right** (**ColNum** + 1) and:
    - Add 1 to its **numDots**
    - Change the value of the cell's **owningPlayer** to the **currentPlayer**
  - Hint: The cell **to the right** is **myGameState. cellArray**(ColNum + 1, RowNum)
- If the exploding cell's **numDots** is now 0, set the **owningPlayer** of that cell to **PLAYER.NONE**
- Call the **CheckForWinner**() function (which you will fill in during the next activity!)

 At this point, your game should be almost complete. Two players can add dots to the board and watch the chain reactions explode!

Lesson Five: Last Link in the Chain

At this point, you should have finished all of the basic functionality for the Chain game. You just need to add some final touches! This lesson describes the last two functions: **CheckForWinner()** and **StopGame()**.

The **CheckForWinner()** function will loop through the cell array and check the ownership of each of the cells. If all of the occupied cells belong to one player, the game is over. In this case, we will refresh the screen one last time and then call the **StopGame()** function.

The **StopGame()** function will simply display a **MsgBox** message congratulating the winner and set **gameOver** = **True**.

Your Turn! Final Touches

In this activity, you will complete the code for the **CheckForWinner()** and the **StopGame()** functions.

CheckForWinner()

The beginning **CheckForWinner()** function has been defined for you in the activity starter.

```
Private Sub CheckForWinner()
```

We have already created two variables for you:

```
Dim player1Alive, player2Alive As Boolean
```

These values will be used to determine if either player still has dots on the board.

To complete this function, you will need to do the following:

- Set **player1Alive** and **player2Alive** to **False**. This assumes neither player has a dot left.
- Create a double **For** loop that will loop through the entire **cellArray**.
- Inside the innermost **For** loop, for each cell:
    - If the **owningPlayer** of the cell is player 1, set the value of **player1Alive** to **True**.
    - If the **owningPlayer** of the cell is player 2, set the value of **player2Alive** to **True**.

Once the double **For** loops are finished, each of your two **Boolean** flags will be set to **True** if the players have at least one dot left on the board. But if one of the flags is **False**, then that player has no dots left and has lost the game!

Next, you need to perform some logic if one of the players has lost the game.

- If the value of **player1Alive** is not equal to **True**, do the following:
  - Call the **Me.Refresh()** function to repaint the screen one last time.
  - Call the **StopGame()** function with **PLAYER.PLAYER2** (since player 2 won the game.)
- If the value of **player2Alive** is not equal to **True**, do the following:
  - Call the **Me.Refresh()** function to repaint the screen one last time.
  - Call the **StopGame()** function with **PLAYER.PLAYER1** (since player 1 won the game.)

StopGame()

Fittingly, the very last function you need to write is **StopGame()**.

```
Private Sub StopGame(ByVal winningPlayer As PLAYER)
```

This function takes only one parameter: the identity of the winning player. To complete this function, you will need to do the following:

- **If** the **winningPlayer** is **PLAYER.PLAYER1**
  - Create a **MsgBox** that indicates that player 1 has won the game. Remember you can use the **player1Description** value.
- **Else** the **winningPlayer** must be **PLAYER.PLAYER2**
  - Create a **MsgBox** that indicates that player 2 has won the game. Remember you can use the **player2Description** value.
- Set the **gameOver** variable to **True** to show that the game is now over!

That's it! At this point your game is fully functional! It can be played by two players and restarted as many times as you like. While the game rules are simple, a winning strategy can be trickier to master. Enjoy!

Lesson Six: Extra Credit

Congratulations! You have completed the final Chain game program! This lesson will just make suggestions for future game enhancements, which you can complete on your own.

Sound Effects

Sounds are a simple, but cool addition to any game. Think about what actions could use some sound: every time the user places a dot? Or maybe when the dots explode? If you need help with this addition, you can take a look back at the Sound chapter and review how we added sounds to the Bubble Blaster game.

Artificial Intelligence

You could add some artificial intelligence to the Chain game. This would make the game one player versus a computer opponent. To add artificial intelligence, you need to figure out the steps that you would take when it was your turn and then apply those same steps in a function that will run when it is the computer's turn. For instance, if you have found that the corner cells are the best cells to "own", you will want the computer to try and place its dots there first. Or you may have found that it is better to have many cells with fewer dots or perhaps better to grow fully populated cell at a time. With some effort you can probably design a computer player that will beat a human player!

Images

You could change the dots that are drawn in the cells with some sort of image or other graphic. Maybe you want to show one dot that gets bigger instead of 1, 2, 3, or 4 dots. Or maybe you want to show an ever-increasing stick of dynamite. The sky's the limit! Use your imagination!

What's Next?

Congratulations, you have finished *KidCoder*^{TM}: *Game Programming*! You now have the fundamental knowledge needed to write your own simple computer games. If you are interested in advancing your skills beyond the Visual Basic language, we encourage you to pursue the other courses available through Homeschool Programming, Inc.

You may also choose to learn other programming languages such as C++, Java, or C#. Each language has strengths and weaknesses which you will discover over time. We offer a *TeenCoder*^{TM} series of courses geared for high school students. These courses will teach you the C# language and also cover game-programming topics using the Microsoft XNA Game Studio.

We hope you have enjoyed this course produced by Homeschool Programming, Inc. We welcome student and teacher feedback at our website. Please also visit our website to request courses on other topics or see what new courses are available!

http://www.HomeschoolProgramming.com